FROM FALLEN TO
FELLOW

HOW A REBELLIOUS YOUTH
STILL BECAME A FELLOW ACTUARY

SONYA ROLANDE, FSA

Edited by: Linda Stubblefield
Cover Design | Print Layout: Kingdom Branding
Cover Image: Shutterstock
Author Photo: Maria Cherkashin Photography

The opinions expressed in this book are those of the author. They are not meant to be political, offensive, or harmful. They also do not necessarily express the viewpoints of anyone or any organization connected to the author. This book reflects the author's present recollections of personal experiences over time. Some names have been changed, some events have been compressed, and some dialogue has been recreated.

Unless otherwise noted, Scripture quotations are taken from the Holy Bible, the New International Version, NIV. Copyright © 1973, 1978, 1984, 2011 by Biblica, Inc. Used by permission of Zondervan. All rights reserved worldwide, www.zondervan.com. The "NIV" and "New International Version" are trademarks registered in the United States Patent and Trademark Office by Biblica, Inc.

ISBN 979-8-9884271-0-0 (Paperback)
ISBN 979-8-9884271-1-7 (Hardcover)
ISBN 979-8-9884271-2-4 (eBook)

Library of Congress Control Number: 2023910128

1st Printing

Printed in the United States of America

To Jesus Christ, my Lord and Savior,
Thank You for rescuing me and
giving me life in abundance!

To my mom and dad,
for your sacrifice and investment in my life,
I thank you! This book is in your honor!

To the youth in inner cities,
Do not let the odds define you.
Rise higher! I believe in you!

Table of Contents

——————

Introduction

————————

I had just been featured in the *Wall Street Journal* for my journey to becoming a Fellow of the Society of Actuaries. Even more so, I was now a Black woman Fellow Actuary. People from around the globe reached out to congratulate me and to let me know that my story had inspired them. I was humbled, but I felt that few knew how much more of my journey needed to be shared. My whole personal story could eventually inspire many more, especially those who looked like me and came from my same basic roots.

My path to becoming a Fellow Actuary would have never even started had I not been shown grace at a time when I nearly self-destructed. I was a rebellious youth who ended up being arrested by the police, but I was given a chance to redeem myself so that one day I could inspire youth living in neighborhoods like the ones in which I grew up. The level I had achieved as a Black Fellow Actuary was not something commonly seen among those of us who grew up in Air-Bel, on the South Side of Chicago, or in L'abbaye.

My journey to beating the odds started with my parents who fought long and hard to open doors of prosperity for my siblings and me. They did everything they could humanly do to ensure our having access to the opportunities they never enjoyed in their careers. They fought for us not to become another number to add to the already negative statistics regarding Black youth living in inner cities. Yet I almost destroyed everything they had sacrificed for me.

I came so close to being labeled a *delinquent*. I became rebellious as I struggled to find my identity between two different worlds—going to school with the elites and then coming home to poverty. I began associating with the wrong crowd to oppose what we saw as injustice. I was missing the bigger picture and purpose, but the graces extended to me led me to find a more excellent and honorable title, that of becoming a Fellow of the Society of Actuaries.

On my journey I learned to fight injustice correctly by staying focused and leading by example. Though I initially experienced many heights on my journey, the inward battle to reach for that title became overwhelming, causing me to spiral into a depression and embrace self-destructive habits. I was not as bright as I had thought and felt like a failure. As I thought about my journey thus far, I questioned my abilities to finish the race for that title. But God picked me up so I could keep on battling for that life my parents had dreamed for me!

Getting this designation was bigger than me. I had come to realize over the many years on this path, from fallen to Fellow, that the greater purpose God had ahead of me would impact generations to come. My life had a higher, greater meaning than reaching this title for myself. I was meant to inspire others and to inspire change like I had been inspired along my journey. We were all meant to live on purpose. This book will move you to rise higher as you extend grace to your world and catch a passion for something greater than yourself. Be blessed as you read!

Sonya Rolande
June 2023

Chapter 1

Angels Still Appear in Prisons

———————

It was a weekday, close to midnight. I had been confined in a prison cell at the police station. I was 16, and my friends with me were about the same age too. We had been caught stealing food at the local grocery store. No, I had not been homeless nor was I starving before this incident.

My mom would leave for her night-shift job around six o'clock in the evening. She worked at a nursing home nearly two hours from our home four or five times a week. A fantastic cook, she always made sure to prepare a meal for us before she left. On this evening, she had cooked steak with potatoes and some veggies. I still recall the smell of the Cameroonian spices she would often put on the meat, and the flavors of the food she prepared were so rich that I almost felt like I was eating without even putting the food in my mouth. She had learned to prepare tasty dishes from all over the world very quickly because of working two jobs. She was often fatigued when she returned home, so she would nap, cook, and prepare for her second job. She never complained about being tired; she loved to feed us. I always found Mom's cooking so comforting. Her care in providing good food reminded us of her when she was working to put food on the table.

That Friday night, when I ended up at the police station, she kissed us all goodbye, told us to eat, and reminded us to do our homework before going to bed. But as soon as Mom left, my neighborhood friends would knock at the door starting on Fridays, and off we would go. She had no idea that I would often sneak away with them on most weekends. Like any concerned mother, Mom would often call us during her break to check on us. Even though I had told my siblings to lie and say that I was sleeping, she eventually found out that I was not home.

I recall dreading the weekends when she would be home in the evening because I could not leave to be with my friends. What did I find so exciting about being outside instead of staying comfortably at home with homemade food? Practically speaking, we couldn't do that much outside, but that time away from the nest gave us a sense of maturity and freedom. We knew very well that we were rebelling against our parents, but we enjoyed the thrill of tasting life without their input.

We were young and "free," and being away from home was cool. Mostly, we would hang out in the neighborhood. We had found a good spot where we would sit for hours to just "kick it," as we would say. The parents of one of my friends were often gone, so we would also hang out at her place. We sometimes enjoyed hanging out at the mall where we found other teenagers like us. We also had "Sunshine," our favorite neighborhood street restaurant where we would hang out if we had enough pocket money to share. If we bought snacks, we would split it evenly as if we were siblings. The ability to buy and share some food gave us all a great sense of family away from home. Our camaraderie made us less homesick. Unfortunately for us, that day we planned far more than we could handle.

I don't know what got into us because we didn't see ourselves as "terrible" troublemakers. One of our greatest fears was getting in trouble while away from home! After all, for most of us, our parents were not aware that we had sneaked out. We only wanted to have some fun hanging out together without getting caught.

We enjoyed each other's company and the laughter we shared. I learned how to come up with and tell jokes from being in that inner circle. We would often sit together and debate about the world, gossip about whatever was trending in our neighborhood, and laugh until we cried. The "only crime" we often committed was being too loud, so people often gave us the *side eye*, which meant "be quiet."

That night, four of my friends—two boys and two girls—came to pick me up at home around 6:30 p.m. I had known Kendra and Betsie for about a year, but they had become "sisters in crime" to me. We had met at a birthday party in an adjacent suburb, Aulnay-Sous-Bois. I went there by train with other friends, but I recall the three of us clicking with each other immediately. We each embraced the same wild spirit.

We wanted to be free from home, explore new things, and make new friends. We were in that season of life when we wanted an early taste of adulthood. Betsie and Kendra were very close friends with Thierry and Ahmed, who had also come with them to pick me up that night. We had become a close circle of friends, and we simply enjoyed each other's daily company. Shortly after leaving my house, Thierry suggested we swing by the mall to meet some of his friends. We did not have a daily agenda for our activities; we simply went with the flow. Before getting to the mall, we had gone to pick up our usual group of friends.

From door to door, we went, making sure our group was complete. That night, I suggested we also pick up my best friend Drea, who, by nature, was a quiet soul and a home nester. She enjoyed staying home to care for her siblings and cook for her family. A year older than me, I considered her more like a big sister.

Drea was not allowed to go outside the house at that time of the day, but we cooked an acceptable scheme for her parents to allow her to go with me. "She will walk me back to my house so we can hang out a little." Of course, I didn't say anything about the others who were with me. I could tell that Drea was uncomfortable hanging out with the other four, but she knew me well and trusted me. After all, we had been friends since I was 12, and since I always considered her the voice of reason, she never expected me to get her into trouble.

Drea was like the perfect daughter my mom may well have wished I was. So having her around reassured me and gave me a sense of security. Having Drea with us meant we would take life more seriously than we usually did. What's sad is that we influenced Drea more than she impacted us that night. In a million years, she could have never thought what happened that night would have happened to her.

We had left home without eating our dinner that day, so we all arrived at the mall hungry. Even Drea had yet to eat the meal she had prepared for her family. I believe they were about to eat when I came to her door to get her. We strolled inside the mall, heading toward the large grocery store. Because we were all walking together as a group, noticing us was not hard. The security guard at the store entrance looked at us strangely, but he still allowed us to come inside. We had no idea we stood out like red flags when we entered the store. Our very presence confirmed their doubts; we meant trouble. That grocery store was the largest in our city with two huge floors divided into sections. We were on the first floor where most of the food and snacks were.

The food must have looked particularly tasty, and we could not restrain our cravings. Thierry went first by taking a box of cookies and opening it as if he had brought it to the mall. He offered it to the next person. At first, the rest of us looked at each other. *Should we take some? We aren't the one who actually first opened the cookies. So what then? It cannot hurt!*

We did not realize that with the bite of a stolen cookie, we also became thieves. With a sense of thrill, we walked around the store, eating and drinking as if we were at home. An indifferent kind of fear combined with the drama of what we were doing. *Will we eventually get caught?* We knew security guards were by the entrance, but they could not see us. Our naive minds had no idea that the store cameras had been centered on us from the moment we walked in!

Honestly, the food only tasted suitable for the few seconds it lasted in our mouths. Swallowing it was bittersweet. Drea refused to eat the food with us. She was terrified at what we were doing, but she thought that as long as she did not eat anything, she wouldn't get in trouble. Little did any of us know that she would be in trouble because of us.

After about ten minutes of eating food items with no intention of paying for them, we all realized our actions had been terribly wrong. Interestingly, Thierry was the first one who decided to leave the store, and we all followed him toward the exit. In this store, we had to take a particular exit line for those leaving without making purchases. The same security guard I had seen at the entrance was now at the exit, and I felt he was staring intensely at me. The truth is, he was looking at our entire group as a whole, but in my guilt, I felt his stare was directed at me alone.

Within seconds, a couple of my friends noticed him...and his fellow security guards who had gathered in the direction we were going. We all knew we had been caught.

I remember having two distinct thoughts: *My mom is going to kill me, and poor Drea...why did I ever involve her in this predicament? Her parents are going to kill her too. We are all heading to jail, and who knows how long we will be there.*

Nevertheless, I still had a sense of security as my "friends" were with me, and at least I would not be alone in facing what was coming. Within seconds, we heard security guards and police officers running toward us, yelling, "Stop and surrender!" That moment was one of the scariest times of my life.

We all were quickly handcuffed and taken to the police truck. I recall seeing the fear and rage in the eyes of onlookers at the store. They probably thought how foolish we were for blatantly stealing, thinking we would face no consequences. I literally felt the intensity of their judgment. The fact that we were all Black kids did not help and only added to our neighborhood's statistics of delinquent youth. The journey to the police station was indeed a frightening one. The handcuffs brought great discomfort, and we had to stay with the officers until a place could be found for us at the station. After we arrived, we were separated.

I can only guess that their plan was to learn who we were, if we had a past record, and then tattle on each other. I thank God that what we had done was our first group trespass; most of us had never been to the police station.

When Drea, Betsie, and I were led to a holding cell, we had no idea where the rest were taken. The cell had urine all over the floor, and the odor was unbearable. Our handcuffs were finally removed, giving us some relief. I couldn't understand why people would urinate in the cell instead of using the toilet until reality kicked in. At about two in the morning, I asked the police guard if I could use the restroom. He took me to an area on the side with a hole, no doors—nothing—no privacy. He stood there and said, "This is the restroom."

I no longer wanted to use the restroom. I now understood implicitly why people used the holding cell instead. When I returned to the *prison cell*, as I called it, Betsie was already gone. Drea told me her aunt had come to pick her up. "My dad is on his way to pick me up," she added. I also learned that reaching my mom had been an issue because she was working the night shift.

The officer said, "You will need to stay until your mom can come get you."

I knew I was in big trouble. Staying in jail felt better than imagining my mom's reaction to seeing me behind bars.

Drea's dad asked for permission to let me go with him so he could drop me at home, but the officer explained, "A parent or legal guardian has to be the one who picks up his or her own child." I was terrified of the idea of staying here without my friends. Reality kicked in once Drea left around four o'clock in the morning. I was now alone in that smelly jail cell.

I didn't need long to reflect on what had happened that day and the countless rebellious days before being caught.

How did I end up here?

Am I that bad of a person?

Am I a rebel, as some like to call me?

What will happen to me if I continue down this route?

Am I setting myself up for failure now and in the future?

These questions and others like them began haunting me as I sat alone in that holding cell. I didn't even know what my future would now look like.

I will have a police record...

I will never be able to achieve some of the dreams my parents had for me.

These thoughts and regrets and others like them were literally killing me inwardly.

I was terrified, and all I wanted to do was rewind the time so that I would have stayed home that night to eat my mom's delicious food instead of lying to her and running out of the house.

Well, Sonya, now it's too late, I thought.

———

One of the police officers came to relay a message. "I have spoken to your mom. She cannot leave work to come get you, so you will need to wait here until an officer can take you home."

I was thankful at the time that he did not share with me what my mom had told him and how she felt. I was already haunted by what she would say when we met face to face and the consequences of my actions.

Not long afterward, another police officer came to take me for questioning about how I had become a delinquent. The tall, white man looked like a "father" to me—an average guy serving his community and ensuring that order remained. To my surprise, he did not look down on me. I had been led to think that police officers had only bad opinions of Black kids, so I was already prepared to be defensive. The media also tended to portray youth living in France inner cities as *racailles*, otherwise known as "scum" in English.

With this man, I did not feel stigmatized or the need to defend myself. I felt a sense of fatherly reassurance in him, like everything would be okay after all. As I sat across from him, answering questions, he attempted to record my answers on his computer. He asked, "What happened that led you to steal food from the store? Did you not have food at home?"

I was so embarrassed to respond because my mom had prepared such a delicious meal that I did not even eat. I ran out of the house as soon as she had left. What a pity! After some time, the police officer stopped typing and looked at me. That's when the father in him became apparent.

"Where are you from? Where do you go to school? Do you even attend school or are you the typical, misbehaving dropout?"

I answered his questions, and I could tell to his surprise, I did not fit the "typical" profile of a Black youth under arrest. I had indeed a different story to tell than that of most of my friends who were caught that day. To provide some context, I lived in a *banlieue* (a "suburb") of Paris named Creteil. More specifically, I lived in L'abbaye, which was considered a *cité de banlieue* ("an inner city"), a large high-density, low-income public housing development that had been built on the outskirts of French cities in the mid-twentieth century. Each banlieue was significantly filled with a population of immigrants and ethnic minorities. By the time my family moved to L'Abbaye, delinquency was at an all-time high among the youth, and significant drug activities made the police label our neighborhood "at risk." L'abbaye had such a bad reputation that most people who ended up there had no other choice. Knowing this history is why the police officer was so stunned by my life story.

Unlike my neighborhood friends, I had the privilege of attending one of the top Parisian high schools. My mom worked two full-time jobs to ensure that she could provide for my siblings and me to attend that private school in downtown Paris. The police officer could not believe it, especially when I told him I was a science student specializing in mathematics in my high school. In France, only the brightest high school students get to enroll in the "series Scientifique," which prepares students for work in scientific fields such as medicine, engineering, and the natural sciences. At first, the police officer thought I was lying. He could not believe I would jeopardize such a bright future over food! My responses embarrassed me because I knew how hard my parents worked to give us a better future. The police officer was so convinced I was lying that he called my mom to tell her what I had said. To his amazement, he soon realized that I was telling the truth, and at that point, he decided to shift gears.

Whether or not I realized at that moment the ultimate stupidity of my actions and how much pain I would cause my parents if my rebellion canceled out their hard work, that police officer did. He put aside his computer and looked me straight in the eyes as if he were my dad. He decided to speak to the depth of my soul, and he gave me some fatherly advice that forever changed the trajectory of my destiny.

"You have the opportunity to become a role model to your friends! They have not had the life of privilege you have lived and the opportunities that have been placed before you. Their parents may not have been able to give them the exposure you have had in private school. They were

———————————

"Young lady, if you get your life straightened out, you could one day make a difference and inspire many Black youths in our city."

———————————

stuck in this bubble of living in this at-risk neighborhood with access to a lower-quality education. The local high school in your neighborhood is known to have a high delinquency rate, with teachers often quitting and students dropping out."

I was aware that many public schools in Creteil and other banlieues faced high levels of poverty and socioeconomic disadvantage, limited resources, and low academic achievement among students.

"Young lady, if you get your life straightened out, you could one day make a difference and inspire many Black youths in our city. You can change for the better, instead of perpetuating the narrative and stigma people have about inner-cities Black kids. You need to use your smart brain to do good and not evil. I believe in you. I can see that you are not really a delinquent; rather, you are just bored out of your mind...and, most likely, a little foolish too."

"I will not put your misbehavior at the grocery store on record nor charge any of you for shoplifting. I will keep your record clean, so your future career opportunities will not be hurt. In return, you must promise me that you will not end up at the police station again."

I made the promise and left his office that day speechless. He and I talked for no more than 15 minutes, but that conversation would forever mark me.

———————

I will never forget that early morning meeting with this police officer. I am still unsure if that man really was an officer or an "angel unawares" who showed up to free me from that literal prison cell as well as from the one of my own making. I had been looking only at myself amid my family and our struggles, but I could not see beyond my problems. I knew that in my rebellion, I was losing so much focus. I had no idea people like me had any worth in the eyes of the police or even within the

French Society. I had been inadvisably focusing on what would only take me to the route of self-destruction.

I suddenly comprehended that police officer was somehow trying to redirect me toward what truly mattered. He showed me that I mattered as a young Black woman, and incredibly, I knew he really believed in me. I can only believe that our meeting was a destiny moment I still see in my mind's eye today. When I left that police station, I now looked at life differently. Somehow, I had found a sense of purpose—something worthy of fighting for instead of rebelling against the status quo. I had been given more than a second chance, and I understood that only a few have enjoyed such turnarounds from their failures.

Above all, he opened my eyes to the fact that I was enjoying some privilege I never thought I had. Not in a million years would I have believed that I could be labeled "privileged," but that officer/angel helped me to see the truth when I had always thought my family was poor and needy. I suddenly saw the hope for people like me or the light at the end of the tunnel. I felt that hope had been planted in my very being, and I could now see living life less subjectively and far more clearly.

When two police officers dropped me at my house, I was still in handcuffs. They only removed the handcuffs at the door once my family confirmed they knew me. What an embarrassment! My siblings had never seen handcuffs that close. They were terrified at the sight of them, but I was somehow at peace now that I was finally home. I am sure my siblings and neighbors thought *the rebel had returned once more from her rebellion.* My siblings had gotten used to my mishaps, but they did not foresee my being in jail.

I felt panicky about what my mother would say to me. Surprisingly, she did not say much. I felt that perhaps that policeman/angel had spoken to my mom and may have convinced her not to scold me because she was very calm. She also stared me in the eyes as he had done, and that directness alone felt like punishment. She basically reiterated the exact words the police officer spoke to me. "Sonya, I know something is very special about you. I know you will make a difference in your world if you could behave."

I had often blocked my ears to Mom's advice as I looked for ways to fight back but not this time. I realized Mom believed so much in her children, and she had sacrificed so much to give us the opportunities she could never attain. I felt the weight of her sacrifices and investment in me. *The time has come for me to rise from the ashes in which I tried to bury myself.*

People who affirm their belief in you are most needed when you doubt your potential, your self-worth, and have reached rock bottom. I was no longer the same after I left that police station. That seed of hope planted in me made me look at life differently. My glimpse of the consequences of a rebellious life had terrified me. I wanted to rise higher. I wanted to rise to the potential that police officer and my mother saw in me. I had found a sense of purpose in their words. At that moment, things clicked.

Perhaps there was a purpose to my growing up the way I did. Others that I could inspire one day may have felt the same way. I no longer felt terrible that I was the only Black girl in my class. Maybe the world was not really racist after all. Maybe there was a purpose to my one day being used to change the statistics of Black youth in *cité*. I wanted to be a *helper* to my friends—not a destroyer. I no longer wanted to be a willing participant in anything that could destroy my future or theirs. I wanted to be someone who would inspire them to believe in themselves the way that officer made me feel. I wanted to reassure those who came to me that they were also worthy and could impact their world for good, contrary to what they or their environment had made them believe. My journey from *fallen* to *Fellow* started when I left that prison cell.

Chapter 2

How My Years of Rebellion Started...

Some of my earliest memories involve my school days in my hometown of Marseille, France. I was five years old, lying flat on my back in the middle of my primary school playground, and I still recall the sky's being bright blue with clouds moving very slowly. I remember being surrounded by the sound of playing and yelling children. During our class break, teachers would take students to the school playground to play. I don't think I had many friends at that time, or I simply did not remember them. I recall being often alone at that age in school.

I was young, but I already had so many existential questions. As I stared at the sky that afternoon, I somehow knew at that moment that there had to be more to my life than just my being there. I already had questions that are probably uncommon for children of that age. I wanted an answer for my existence.

Who is out there in these bright skies?

Why do I feel such a drawing to pay attention to what's beyond?

Is there a God out there?

If He is real, does He see me?

Why did He leave me here alone?

Why didn't He make me like everyone else?

These were only a few of my beginning questions. I had many more, and I would have liked to discuss them with Him.

———————

Marseille is the second most populous city in the south of France. A major center for immigrant communities from former French colonies, Marseille enjoys a diverse population. Growing up, I enjoyed the friendship of many from North African countries as well as other African countries. For the most part, if I had asked my friends where they were from, three out of four of them would have said they were originally from either Algeria, Morocco, or Tunisia. Though race may seem trivial to many, ethnicity already mattered to me. I always felt different growing up and somehow never fit the mold. I did not have the long, curly, or straight hair like most of my classmates. Neither did I have lighter, tanned skin or colored eyes. These attributes mattered to my little self. Little did I know I was privileged to experience the diversity of cultures at such a young age. The richness of culture and traditions of the people with whom I lived greatly impacted my early view of the world.

I was born in Marseille, and not long after my birth, my parents moved to a neighborhood in Marseille named Air-Bel. Built in the late 1970s, Air Bel was a neighborhood in the eleventh district of Marseille. Over the years, Air-Bel had developed a terrible reputation for social and economic problems, including poverty, unemployment, and crime. The area became an economically deprived community, replete with low-income housing projects (HLMs), a term I had often heard at home. We lived in an HLM, and most people who interacted with my parents lived in the same circumstances. Our world, and therefore, my world, centered around living in an HLM neighborhood.

Due to its architecture, Air Bel, often referred to as a "labyrinth" neighborhood, consisted of four towers and small buildings arranged in a hexagonal shape. In France, many subsidized buildings were distinct as they were tall and could probably house hundreds of families. I lived in one of the small buildings with five floors. The buildings in our area all looked the same. The city probably hired the same architect to create the concept for our entire community. The designs were kept simple in shape but were creative with the paint. The city would often repaint Air-Bel's buildings every other year with bright colors. I used to love the colors of those buildings and how they were maintained then. Perhaps keeping them painted was a way to add sunshine to some of the people who endured many struggles in those communities. The only caveat was the beauty of these buildings would quickly shed away with occasional fires, most often from leaking gas pipes, graffiti, or the natural erosion of the paint.

I clearly remember the four identical, very tall towers in Air-Bel that always terrified me as a child. I was deathly afraid of heights and could not imagine what standing on the balcony of one of these high floors would be like. The very thought terrified me.

For some reason, I was also intrigued by a group of young people hanging around day and night at the bottom of these tall towers. I was probably seven years old before I finally realized what they were doing. By then I learned that these were drug dealers who had their spots at the building entrance or the street corners. Familiarizing myself with the smell of their merchandise did not take long. I knew the smell of marijuana from a young age, but I did not know what it was then. As much as I became comfortable living in Air-Bel, I somehow knew something was off with my little world. Yet I somehow assumed my world looked the same as everywhere else.

––––––––––

Her name was like mine, except hers was spelled with an "i"—Sonia, whereas mine was spelled with a "y." I believe she was of Algerian descent, with her brownish-green eyes, and her long, silky brown hair with blonde highlights. Sonia, whose building was adjacent to mine, was my neighbor and my first friend. She often knocked at my door around seven or eight o'clock on the weekends. I was an early bird myself, so I enjoyed her company. However, my siblings did not like her visits since they enjoyed sleeping in on Saturdays.

Most of the time when Sonia knocked, my mom had already left the house for work, and we were often home alone on Saturdays. I was not supposed to open the door, one of the safety measures Mom had put in place to keep us safe while she worked. The truth is we were way too young to stay home alone, but she had no choice but to work to provide for our needs. Mom did her best to ensure that while she was away from home, we were all safe from danger. We understood the importance of never going out while she was gone.

Unfortunately, I was already beginning to develop a rebellious spirit. I hated being stuck at home. Something about being outside created a sense of thrill and adventure in me. Being home often brought memories of loneliness and boredom. My siblings, who were primarily very calm introverts were there with me, but they did not really like noisy environments or crowded spaces.

I was very different from them in character; in fact, I was their opposite. I enjoyed the noise and connecting with others outside the house. So when Sonia knocked on our door on Saturdays, I would toss away every instruction my mom had given us and would leave to play in our hood. Sonia and I formed an early habit in life of sneaking out.

Some might wonder what seven-year-olds were doing outside on their own, but seeing little kids unsupervised was pretty much the norm in Air-Bel. You would think people would have asked or cared to know what children our age were doing. I was accustomed to seeing children my age walking the streets. I am unsure if all those kids I saw had also sneaked out or if their parents somehow trusted that "the streets" were safe for their children. Most of the families I knew somehow trusted each other and felt their kids would be okay just hanging out not too far from home. Perhaps they could see us from the windows. If these kids were sneaky like me, they were likely looking for greener pastures away from home. For the most part, we always felt safe outside and never had anyone stalk us. At that young age, I didn't have a sense of what danger was or could be. Sonia and I longed for something to add excitement and joy to our little worlds.

Sonia's parents were busy like my mom and rarely home. Sonia was privileged to have both parents living with her, whereas I only had my mom. I often arrived at her place to find only Sonia and her younger brother in the apartment. She would also break the "Do-not-open-the-door-to-strangers" rule. The fact that we both pushed our boundaries may have been the reason why we liked each other so much. We were "partners-in-crime" who longed for something more.

Even when my mother was at home, she was often busy getting things ready for the next day. As a result, I did not feel a closeness to her that would have made me yearn to stay home. I was too young to understand why she was away so often, why she could not stay still. I would often stand by the balcony to watch her hurry off to work. She would often wave goodbye to me, and even at that distance, I could see the guilt in her eyes.

My mom had no other choice. She did her best to make our world joyful with home-cooked meals, snacks, and a television. She taught us how to use the microwave to warm our food and always instructed us never to turn on the gas range in the kitchen. My mom's worst nightmare was coming home to fire and flames. Thank God I never felt the need to disobey that instruction.

Nevertheless, my mother knew I was sometimes adventurous and wild and often called me "Mommy Catastrophe." I could not stay still like my siblings, and I hated the feeling of being bored. Unfortunately, home was often boring to me. As much as Mommy loved on us when she was around, to me she always seemed to be on the go, and I remember the void I felt more than her cuddles.

My dad's absence added to that emptiness I often felt at home. I grew to hate the feeling of being stuck at home because too often it magnified the realities of what I lacked. Escaping the nest was my way of forgetting where I came from and the deep sense that my family was somehow inadequate. Sonia probably shared some of the same feelings I battled with. More than likely, some of the kids with whom we associated outside the walls of "home" also felt the emptiness.

Sonia's parents would often fight, and I know the unrest in her home impacted her. Most times when I knocked at her door, I saw fear in her eyes. She was a different Sonia at home than the one with whom I played outside. I often felt that she wanted to run away. Seemingly, we all wanted something that would bring light into our children's world.

Behind our buildings was an average-size playground with plenty of grass. In the middle, we could play on swings and enjoy other games. We could skate or run down a steep walkway surrounding the playground. Sonia and I loved being at that playground. Most of the time, we would lay down on the grass and talk about nothing and everything. Sonia also enjoyed staring at the sky as I did. We would lay down quietly side by side, simply staring at the sky above.

Since the playground was not directly visible from our house, Mom needed to go outside to look through the staircase to check on my siblings and me. Neither was Sonia's building visible from the playground, so her parents also came outside to check on her. Having our parents checking on us didn't matter much since we would go there even when they were not home. That playground was our go-to place—our little heaven away from home.

Neither Sonia nor I had money to buy snacks or tidbits like chewing gum. We developed a certain fascination with chewing gum. We would stare at people with gum and try to imagine what they were feeling by the way they chewed their gum. From watching them, we thought chewing gum would be so cool. We wanted to experience those feelings too, so we hatched a scheme to get some gum.

Candy and gum were considered expensive commodities when I was growing up—or so I thought. My neighborhood had a French bakery called a *boulangerie* and most of them sold candies. This one in Air-Bel was located close to my school. Sonia and I often dreamt that we would have enough money to buy all the goods we wanted from the boulangerie. To describe the joy I felt every time I saw or passed by that store is indescribable. Every item I could see through the glass windows fascinated me. After school, I would often walk by to stare at the people walking in and out, and, of course, to stare at the delicious candies.

Our desire to chew gum was so strong and since our parents could not afford to take us to the boulangerie, Sonia and I decided to pick up discarded gum we found on the ground. We would take these used pieces of gum to my house and wash them carefully. After all, washing the gum would remove any germs and make it safe to chew. We would then chew the pieces as if they were new.

We knew what we were doing was disgusting and bizarre, but we finally had that coveted gum to chew. We took the gum to school so our friends could see that we were cool—like the people we had watched. Where Sonia and I got our gum was our little secret. Unfortunately, that habit of picking up gum from the ground evolved into another more interesting one that was far more dangerous.

Smoking cigarettes has a long history in France. In the 90s, forty percent of the adult population smoked. I actually think that statistic was much higher in Air Bel. To my little eyes, seemingly two out of three people smoked cigarettes in my hometown. Sonia's parents smoked at home, and I remember always smelling cigarettes in her house. My mom did not smoke but given that smoking was an everyday occurrence in our neighborhood, I had become accustomed to the habit. Teachers and parents smoked outside of schools, people smoked at the bus stop, and people smoked on my way to and from our house. Smoking at that time in Marseille was normal to do, and cigarettes were everywhere.

Over time, smoking became more widespread, especially after the mass production of cigarettes in the early twentieth century. In France, cigarettes were sold in *tabac*, and the tabac in my neighborhood was next door to the boulangerie. I always knew only adults entered them, and that children were forbidden to smoke. However, Sonia and I were not only fascinated by cigarettes, but we were also mesmerized with how people would hold and smoke their cigarettes. We started playing with fake paper, pretending that we were adults smoking and discussing important topics. My interest in cigarettes then morphed into something else. I then wanted to experience what it was like to blow smoke out of my mouth like I watched so many adults do.

One day at home, I made a cigarette out of paper, found some matches, and lit my fake cigarette. I remember trying that first "cigarette" like yesterday. The smell was horrible—nothing like the cigarettes I knew from outside. However, I loved trying to replicate blowing that smoke from my mouth. I did not inhale it; I held the smoke in my mouth and blew it out.

My mom happened to be home that day, and I was alone in my room with the door closed. I had opened the windows wide so she would not smell the odor. Unfortunately for me, she did.

I heard her yell from the living room, "Sonya, what is that smell coming from your room?" I quickly extinguished my burning "cigarette" and threw it out the window. I suddenly became terrified at the idea of

Mom catching me "smoking."

When she barreled into my room, she looked around, searching for what I could have been doing but saw no evidence of my misdeed. After all, how could a mother possibly think her seven-year-old daughter could create a fake cigarette and smoke it in her house? Since Mom had never smoked, the idea that I would try was unthinkable to her.

When I shared with Sonia what I had done, I told her every detail of my experiment and how cool it was to see the smoke coming from my mouth. Sonia was absolutely fascinated by my rendition of smoking.

I could tell she wanted me to create another fake cigarette with her so we could experience "smoking" together. Sonia came up with an even bigger plan than I had imagined, proposing that we pick up partially smoked cigarettes on the ground and smoke them!

I thought she had a genius idea, and I was eager to execute her plan. The next time we went to the playground, we walked around looking for half-consumed cigarettes and found a perfect one by the staircase where Sonia lived. Not only did we find a "perfect" cigarette, but we also found the perfect location to smoke inside the staircase where we wouldn't be seen. In preparation for our initiation to try the real thing, I had brought the matches from my house.

Sonia held the cigarette, and I lit it using the match. She tried it first, and then I tried it as well. Even though we coughed intensely, we did not stop puffing on the cigarette. To us, we had graduated from being boring kids. We felt like adults and thought smoking was fascinating and cool. Seeing people smoke was so common in our world that we knew we would eventually join the club. Doing it earlier than expected was the excitement we were looking for to have an early taste of our future. We coughed a lot and were scared we would get caught, but we enjoyed the moment while it lasted.

Interestingly, or some would say *thankfully*, our first cigarette was our last until years later. That cigarette we smoked on that staircase was the only one we tried together. As I look back at this experience, I believe we felt as if we had undergone a rite of passage and then lost interest in smoking cigarettes. Perhaps the uncomfortable coughing or the deception and effort needed made us lose interest, and maybe we would try again when we became adults.

DISCLAIMER
AGAINST SMOKING

Cigarette smoking leads to disease and disability and harms nearly every organ of the body. Smoking causes cancer, heart disease, stroke, lung disease, type 2 diabetes, and other chronic health conditions. The impact on a pregnant woman or breathing secondhand smoke extends beyond the smoker. This book in no way encourages smoking and strongly advises quitting now to reduce severe health risks dramatically. Please consult with a medical professional to seek help with quitting. If you know any child exposed to indiscriminate smoking, please contact your local child protection authority.

Looking back on these times, I am amazed that young children could be left alone to make so many potentially dangerous decisions as the ones I made. However, that choice was one of the consequences children faced in our part of the world with parents who worked long hours to ensure their family's survival. Even with working multiple jobs, people in Air-Bel needed better pay and reasonable work hours. Many were only earning minimum wage.

I had heard my mom use the term *minimum wage* during some of her phone conversations as well as with people who visited our home. In France, minimum wage was known as the SMIC, i.e., *Salaire minimum interprofessionnel de croissance*. Because Mom was supporting a family of five, she worked many extra hours to meet our needs. The SMIC was insufficient for her to work regular hours and spend adequate time with her children.

Many families would complement their source of employment with government funding and benefits. However, Mom always refused to collect money from the government. She addressed this matter at home and how essential it was to fight to leave this "dependency system." She took great pride in working hard not to be dependent on anyone. She hated the feeling of being caged in the public housing system of HLMs. My mother believed that if she worked hard enough, she would escape that environment. Her goal was to fight to financially secure her children's freedom from a life of constant struggle. She could pay the bills and provide for her children by herself, which gave her a sense of dignity and pride that allowed her to keep her head high, despite the socio-economic issues she noticed daily in our neighborhood.

My time away from home continually exposed me to adult situations no child should ever know exists. Perhaps most seven-year-olds in Air-Bel weren't being exposed to pornography, but I had to wonder if it happened to others when my friend introduced me to that world of filth. I still recall the first time I was shown a pornographic magazine.

I was playing in the playground right after school on a night my mom happened to be home. She allowed me to go to the playground to enjoy the companionship of other children. Sonia was not around that day, but then her parents did not usually allow her to go out when they were home. Some of my other classmates lived in the building near me, and Jessica was in the same class as me. She had silky, curly dark hair and very dark brown eyes. She had a younger sister and a younger brother. Though I would not have considered Jessica a close friend, we would sometimes play at the playground since we were neighbors.

Jessica was playing with me when her mom called from their balcony to come home for dinner. Jessica's mom was single, raising her three children in Air-Bel. From what Jessica had shared with me, they were accustomed to moving around frequently. They had moved to Air-Bel not that long ago. Her home faced the playground, so her mom could easily supervise Jessica and her siblings.

For some reason, Jessica asked me to come with her to her house. Since I was also inquisitive, I wanted to see what her house looked like. So, I followed her home. When we arrived at her house, she took me to her room, where she stayed with her siblings. The meal wasn't quite ready, so she still had some free time before I left. We sat down on the edge of her bed, and with wide-open eyes and a twisted smile, she said, "Sonya, I have something to show you."

Her siblings were still in the room, and given they were younger than us, I assumed what she would share with me would be innocent. How wrong I was! From a hidden spot inside her closet, she pulled out a magazine. I was only familiar with one that listed televisions programs by channels for the week. I had also seen magazines displayed outside the tabac, but I never really paid any attention to them. Given that children were off-limits from the tabac, I associated magazines with adult reading.

When Jessica dug out that magazine, I knew instinctively that she had something she had no business having. She sat next to me at the edge of her bed and opened the magazine pages to the section she was eager for me to see.

I had never seen such sights. "Sonya," she jokingly whispered in a low voice, "I stole the magazine! We've all been looking at it ever since."

I was so uncomfortable, knowing her mother was home and could open her bedroom door at any moment and catch us. Worrying about being caught bothered me so much that I could not focus on the magazine. I did not understand what I was seeing, but what I did see disturbed me. I knew within me that something was very wrong. I felt like part of my innocence was ripped from me when Jessica showed me that magazine. The more I was away from home, the more I kept spiraling downward, ingesting more and more depravity.

DISCLAIMER
AGAINST PORNOGRAPHY

For children to be given access to pornographic content is illegal. Exposure to pornography at a young age may lead to poor mental health, sexism and objectification, sexual violence, and other negative outcomes. This book in no way encourages watching pornographic content. If you know any child exposed to such, please contact your local child protection authority.

If exposure to smoking and pornography was not enough for a seven-year-old girl, violence was yet another horror to which I was exposed early on at Air-Bel. Sonia and I shared a mutual "friend," Cruela, who was of the same Algerian origin as Sonia. I believe their mothers were acquaintances, which is how the two girls had become close friends. In school, they often jokingly referred to one another as *cousins.*

Sonia was not as close to Cruela as she was to me. Losing her mother the previous year had seemed to turn Cruela into a very unhappy girl. She had been displaying aggressive behavior in school, often fighting with other students. In our primary school, the fights were brutal. Students would even schedule fights for after school. At the school entrance, students would wait outside to see who would win the fight, which would then become a discussion topic in class. In rare instances, students would relocate a heated fight to the school playground, and teachers would have to separate them. I had watched Cruela fight with another student who had made fun of her. I always wondered why Cruela was so angry all the time and never smiled.

Cruela's harsh behavior made me wonder why Sonia even paid attention to her. I knew that Cruela publicly ridiculed Sonia, calling her stupid. Sonia had fallen behind the previous year, so her teachers made her repeat the class. I was a year younger than Sonia, but I had skipped a grade, which is why we were in the same class the previous year. I was now in third grade with Cruela, but I always avoided her in class because she was so spiteful.

One day while we were on the playground, Cruela slapped Sonia in front of me for no reason. She quickly tried to excuse what she had done by saying, "I was only joking," but Sonia started crying and came to me.

"Cruela," I yelled, "I will report you to our parents and teachers!"

She immediately reacted by cursing and yelling, "I will beat you after school!" She went a step further and told our entire class that we would be fighting right after class.

I was so anxious because I had never been involved in any physical violence before. I knew my mom would not come to pick me up from school, so I also knew I was on my own. My siblings did not know how to fight either, and out of the three of us, I had the best chance of winning the upcoming fight.

True to her word, Cruela waited for me outside school that day. I did my best to avoid her, but she stepped in front of me, pushed me around, and insisted that I fight her. When she started pulling my hair, I started yanking hers too. Thankfully, a group of older students finally separated us.

As I was about to run to my house in tears to avoid creating a greater scene, a teacher who saw us fighting from afar came quickly to confront us. "Girls, I will be calling your parents to let them know you were fighting on school property," she said.

I immediately started crying because I had never engaged in violent behavior or seen violence so up close.

As soon as Mom came home, I told her what happened. I explained that I was defending my friend Sonia against Cruela who then insisted on fighting me. "Mom, she could have hurt me badly if I had not defended myself."

I was so thankful Mom believed me. After all, my mischievous, inquisitive spirit had led me astray enough times that Mom had reason not to believe me. She talked to the school principal about what had transpired, and Cruela was expelled for a few days. She was also banned from approaching me at school.

The sad part of living in Air-Bel was becoming accustomed to the violence happening around us. Seeing fights outside of my school was common. Cruela's trying to fight me was not a singular incident. Kids were frequently exposed to fighting and violence—even in primary school at Air-Bel. My first exposure to what violence looked like frightened me. I felt like I had lost another part of my innocence at such a very young age.

"My environment also played a role in influencing my actions and perpetuating a vicious cycle of poverty, parental absence, youth delinquency, violence, dangerous exposures and so forth."

DISCLAIMER
AGAINST VIOLENCE

No violence against and among children is acceptable. This book in no way condones violence in any venue. Such exposure in children can cause significant physical, mental, and emotional harm with long-term effects that can last well into adulthood. Exposure to violence can limit a child's potential and increase his or her likelihood of being charged by the juvenile or criminal justice system. If you know any child exposed to violence, please contact your local child protection authority.

I believe there is always a beginning to bad behavior. In my case, my uncontrolled and dangerous curiosity and easily influenced personality drew me into inappropriate situations. I developed rebellious tendencies that led to my ignoring parental instructions and doing as I pleased without considering the consequences. My mother tried her best effort to tame me, but she could only do so much. This disregard for authority led me to be exposed to dangerous habits and practices.

My environment also played a role in influencing my actions and perpetuating a vicious cycle of poverty, parental absence, youth delinquency, violence, dangerous exposures and so forth. Statistics uphold the known fact that children who are not supervised and left to themselves will be more likely to engage in rebellious activities. Studies have shown that children who grow up without the presence of a parent or a caregiver may be at a higher risk for engaging in delinquent behavior. Research has also shown that parental absence, especially during critical developmental stages, can increase the likelihood of problem behaviors such as substance abuse, criminal activity, and behavioral issues.

As much as correcting destructive behavior in children is essential, identifying and correcting the underlying issues that may influence such actions and repetitive cycles is also necessary.

As I look back and examine the past, I have been able to identify patterns leading to delinquency that could be corrected in the lives of children or systems or environments in the future. Delinquency rates in a neighborhood like Air-Bel were often much higher than in other areas of Marseille.

My mom had already noticed negative patterns in our neighborhood youth. She also saw those young teenagers selling drugs on street corners and engaging in criminal activities. She had seen the police arrest them and then take them to juvenile prison. Delinquency and lawlessness were emblazoned in the daily news. She knew our exposure to such destructive behavior and influences could eventually manifest in us. Her primary motivation every time she had to leave us home alone to go to work was part of her daily fight to beat the odds. Mom was determined to get us out of that environment with continuous high-level delinquency statistics. She knew she would need to fight hard to ensure we did not end up on those street corners too.

Little did she know the clock was already ticking because I was the one becoming that ticking bomb.

Chapter 3

My Family's Fight to Beat the Odds

I was seven years of age when I saw what battling *adversity* looked like. Until then, I had no point of reference to determine whether my life was really abnormal. I had erroneously assumed the world outside of Air-Bel was the same as mine. In my young mind, more than likely, people everywhere looked the same. The buildings in which we all lived looked the same. Children acted the same. No doubt, other parents worked the same schedule as mine did. I just thought life was the same everywhere, but somehow, I did aspire for more than Air-Bel.

I remember standing by the bathroom window on a sunny Saturday, waiting for my mom to return. The sky was light blue with beautiful clouds perfectly shaped. A refreshing breeze helped cool my body from the heat. Located on the Mediterranean coast in the south of France, Marseille enjoyed mild, wet winters and warm, dry summers. Mommy had gone out very early that morning, but she had promised she would not be gone long, so I was waiting patiently to welcome her back home. I enjoyed window watching, staring outside for hours, wondering what other people's lives were like. From the vantage point of that window, things were fairly quiet that Saturday morning. Usually, we would hear the sound of cars and people speaking loudly when calling to a family member from their windows.

I usually woke up early on Saturdays, and that Saturday, I caught Mom right before she was about to leave. Once she left, I enjoyed a biscotti with jam, and I made hot chocolate with milk and powder. After eating, I played alone, entertaining myself. I was used to playing by myself early in the mornings, or I would go out to play with Sonia, but she did not come looking for me that morning.

I shared a room with my younger sister, so I played in the living room to let her sleep. Many times, my solitary playing consisted of being the mom of the house. I would clean the house, reorganize items, sweep, and mop the floor. I would mimic what I had watched Mom do. She had nicknamed me "Miss Catastrophe" because my cleaning generally consisted of turning the house upside down. I cannot say she was ever a fan of my cleaning abilities then.

When the time came for Mom to return, I decided to stand by the window that faced the bus station—where I knew I would see her walking toward home. I assumed she was coming back from her other full-time job. On Saturdays, she worked as a cleaning lady and caretaker for an older woman, but that woman did not need her that afternoon. I stood by the window, waiting for her to return home.

The sun was shining very bright that day when I finally saw my mom from afar. I could recognize her from miles away. She was not tall, and I knew that she was wearing a dark blue top with what looked like black pants. I could tell Mom was perspiring because her face was shining brightly. She was carrying what looked like loads of groceries—at least five or six bags in each hand.

She must have gone to the supermarket right after work.

It was already close to two o'clock in the afternoon when she finally returned. My mother was a powerful woman, often carrying home heavy bags filled with groceries for the week. She walked to the bus stop 15 minutes from our apartment, and she carried heavy bags 15 minutes back home from the bus stop.

I was overjoyed to see her. My mother was a beautiful woman with a perfect smile, and I always loved looking at her; her presence was invariably reassuring. She made me feel less alone because we were often home alone.

My mom saw me smiling at her in the window and returned that smile with her perfect one. For the first time ever, I saw my mom carrying groceries from a distance. She would generally already be at the door when she brought in the groceries. I had never seen her perspiring so much. This time her arrival home was different; something was off. Everything somehow seemed abnormal...but then something clicked.

My childish understanding of life began to take shape. I knew life was not supposed to be this way. I felt it in her eyes. Even thought I could identify strength and determination in her face, I realized carrying these bags had to weigh heavily on her. Suddenly, I could see the toll on her body and soul as well as the sacrifices she was making for us. Mommy kept pushing with every step she took toward the house.

For the first time in my mind's eye, I captured what sacrifice and resilience looked like. I also realized what *adversity* looked like—at least from my child's point of view. I saw in my mom's walk, her eyes, and even in her soul the battle she wrestled daily to get home that day and every day to secure a place for her children. Her sweat represented all that she was fighting on our behalf.

My mom was determined to ensure that our future would be brighter than her past. She would not allow us to become common statistics of the youth in Air-Bel. She was determined to beat these odds. I read all that on her face that day. Mom would never speak to us about her difficulties at home. I knew she worked a lot, and I partially understood the significance of what she was doing for us. I saw parts of her struggle and pain in striving to achieve more for us. Those heavy grocery bags represented the price she was willing to pay and the lengths she would go to achieve her goal. That day as I watched Mom from that window,

"I saw in my mom's walk, her eyes, and even in her soul the battle she wrestled daily to get home that day and every day to secure a place for her children."

I knew what fighting against adversity looked like, and her resilience marked me.

I ran to the door to welcome her back. In France, we kiss each other's cheeks. Personal touch was always my love language, and while growing up and even into my adulthood, I always greeted my mom by kissing her on the lips. After I greeted her, she unloaded the groceries in the kitchen. I hugged her as a way of thanking her for her sacrifice. I wanted to somehow relieve her pain. "*Mom, in the future, could you take me to the grocery store so I can help you carry the bags?*"

I knew I didn't want her to fight alone any longer. That day I saw how hard it was for her to battle alone. Now I was determined to join her in the fight. No one had verbally defined adversity for me; I somehow knew instinctively that intangible called *adversity* was our enemy.

Mom looked at me, maybe with a hint of guilt in her eyes, and responded, "*Okay, I will take you with me to the grocery store from now on.*"

———

My parents were in their early twenties in the mid-80s when they relocated to France from Cameroon as university students. Some of Cameroon's brightest students could receive scholarships from the government to study abroad in France. My dad had received a scholarship to complete his Ph.D. in Economics from the Université d'Aix-Marseille. Mom followed my dad to complete her bachelor's degree in the Science of Education. Poverty was a major issue in Cameroon that affected a significant portion of the population, including my parents. Both grew up poor, and their parents struggled to provide for their families.

Nevertheless, their parents had instilled in them two critical fundamentals from an early age: *faith and the importance of education*. They learned how to face difficulties without giving up. They had learned not to be afraid of challenges, and they both learned how to work hard at a young age to help their parents. The odds of rising higher were not in their favor, but they still had faith that their tomorrow would somehow be better. They grew up joyful amid adversity.

Stories my parents shared about their upbringing were always filled with laughter. They did not focus on the bitter tears life brought their way. My parents valued education and hard work despite the challenges they faced growing up, which is why they positioned themselves for opportunities to travel abroad to countries such as France. Because France had a long history of providing high-quality education, my parents felt moving there would help them improve their knowledge and potentially increase their prospects for the future.

Together, my parents had plans to build a better future for themselves and dreamed of having their children live in wealth and love, benefiting from the fruits of their labors. Coming to France was a very long-awaited dream. In their early years of living in France, they took many photographs. In many of these pictures, they seemed joyful—kissing, hugging, and smiling at what they thought would be ahead of them. It even looked as if they had made it. However, little did they know that adversity would continue to haunt them.

The tides did not turn in their favor, and upon completing his Ph.D., opportunities did not open for my dad to stay in France. In order to provide for his family, he returned to Cameroon to work. My parents assumed their children's future would be better if we remained in France with my mom. My mom never imagined that she would end up raising us alone in France while my dad lived thousands of miles away in Cameroon.

Unfortunately, almost immediately upon my father's arrival in Cameroon, he met with disastrous news. The company that had hired him could not pay him the promised salary, so my dad was unable to provide for our family as he had hoped. Mom was left to be the sole provider for our family in France. Returning to Cameroon was not a viable option in Mom's mind. Allowing us to live the life of poverty she had known was unimaginable to her. Despite France's challenges, she knew staying was much better than returning to Cameroon.

I was always intrigued about why my parents, even with all their degrees, did not find success in their careers at that time in France. When I questioned Mom, she responded, with much disappointment in her voice, "Things were different in France then. We didn't know people who could help us rise in French society, and we knew we needed to familiarize ourselves with the system."

I know of no single reason why educated Black immigrants struggled to succeed in France in the 1990s. Clearly my parents had to cross the barriers of cultural differences and had limited access to social and professional networks for support and mentoring. In that time, with the French economy struggling, unemployment was high, making it difficult for many people, including immigrants, to find good jobs. As much as my parents met great people who welcomed them into French society, they did not have people to mentor them to their next level of success in France. They did not come from a family that could open doors of opportunities for them in France.

My parents had to create these career opportunities independently, which they found difficult to achieve with young children. As a result, my mother paused her career pursuit to meet the immediate needs of her home. Yet this setback did not extinguish her fire for success. She may not have attained success in her career, but she was determined to open doors of opportunities for her children. Mom carried those grocery bags with that fire in her eyes. Whether the job required a degree or no degree, she was ready to work to the core to create a better world for us. She would not allow her environment or circumstances to dictate her children's future. She was determined to beat the odds.

———————

While in Cameroon, my father was also looking for ways to support our family. My parents had not left Cameroon with their future dreams and ambitions for their family to end in Air-Bel. Life in Air-Bel was different from the vision they had for their future. Air-Bel was not the France of their dreams nor the future they had dreamed for their children. Their dreams centered around owning their own home and traveling around France during holidays to learn about French culture and heritage. They wanted to embrace the France they were told about while growing up in Cameroon.

Unfortunately, the life we were living in France looked nothing like their hopes and dreams. Being stuck in Air-Bel seemed like a curse to them. Since France did not give them the opportunities they had dreamt of, they were ready to move on. Unknown to me then, my parents had discussed relocating to another country. My parents had heard stories of African families enjoying great success in the United States. They had heard stories of Africans in the United States starting successful businesses, or attending college and finding jobs in their field of expertise.

How can someone with an earned Ph.D. end up struggling? My parents had seen immigrants with graduate degrees in France struggle to make ends meet, and living that same struggle was a painful reality for them. These success stories they heard about Africans in the United States were enticing to my parents. Growing up in Marseille, I had yet to see a "successful" Black family. *Never!* In my small world, how I defined *success* was based on my mom's discussions about what she aspired to do. Mom often said she wanted to own her own home and not live in public housing. Her definition became mine—owning our own home and car.

All the people we knew were struggling like our family and living where we lived in the same public housing. People like us dreamt of home ownership in Air-Bel but had yet to achieve that dream. So, my dad decided to apply for the Green Card Lottery to come to the United States. Emigrating to America became my parent's new utopia. Because the opportunities for success in France seemed unachievable to them, they gave up that dream.

I will never forget that call that came on a Saturday afternoon. Mom was cleaning the house, and she was about to finish mopping the floor. My siblings and I were all sitting on the couch with snacks in hand, watching a kids' movie. We were comfortable and happy on that day. Mom was about to mop the floor under our feet near the couch, so we raised our feet for her. Right then, the phone rang. Mom put everything aside and went to answer the phone in the hallway.

A door separated the hall from the living room, but she did not shut the door. I could hear some of the conversation. I noticed her voice sounded different—joyous and hopeful was the only way I can describe it. After 15 to 20 minutes of speaking on the phone, she called for us to come. I was the first one to get to her. I was curious to know who was on the phone with her.

I picked up the phone and heard what I thought was the voice of my dad. To me, I felt like an eternity had passed since I had last spoken to him, and I didn't really remember what his voice sounded like. Most of his calls were limited to speaking to Mom.

I don't recall having many conversations with him, so that call felt special. Dad asked me how I was doing and quickly told me with excitement that he would be returning to France to stay with us. I was so excited, and at the same time, felt so reassured that we would no longer have to be home alone. *Daddy would be here with us!* After that call, I saw a smile and a look of peace on my mom that day, which made me believe that great news was coming. My dad's coming brought us great joy, and I counted the days with excitement. We could all sense a brighter future ahead.

Dad returned to France in 1997 when I was nine years old. I recall him seating all the family at the table to discuss some "big news." He shared that he had received a letter confirming that our family had won the Green Card Lottery to move to the United States. On the day Dad had called, he had told my mom the news though she had chosen not to share this news with us. She wanted Dad to tell us. I had no idea that Dad was coming to take us away from Air-Bel.

I had only heard of the United States through movies, so I thought all the celebrities we saw in movies lived there. I also thought only the very, very rich lived in America. Going to America did not seem attainable for people like us. I thought we were stuck forever in Air-Bel. After all, we did not have a car, and I knew the bus couldn't possibly go that far. We only took the bus with Mom to the grocery store or the doctor's office.

Dad explained that we would travel by train to the American Embassy in Paris to collect our United States green cards before returning to Marseille. From there we would depart by plane to go to the United States. The concept of taking the train, let alone a plane, was foreign to me. I felt sad and immediately thought of Sonia. I did not want to leave her, and the idea of having to make new friends frightened me. Dad also told us that we would now need to learn English. Suddenly the good news felt very burdensome.

My brother was super excited as he had learned about the United States in school and was far more familiar with that country. In reality, my brother only knew about American cars and limousines. His dream was to see a limousine, which he could already describe with great joy.

Getting ready to leave happened very quickly. From the time Dad came to France from Cameroon until when we left for the United States was about eight months. We became instant celebrities in town. When our neighbors in Air-Bel learned we were moving to the United States, our leaving seemingly brought hope of a better tomorrow to many people and gave them something to strive for besides living in Air-Bel. Everyone's cheers and best wishes encouraged us, bringing excitement about our upcoming journey.

I thought that we would arrive in the United States, be picked up by a limousine, and turn into instant celebrities like I saw in the movies. We would become automatically rich. My mom would no longer struggle, we would own beautiful cars, and live in a big house we owned. I was already dreaming of what I thought would become our reality. Since my parents did not have the finances to travel, they took a loan to be able to pay for the train tickets to Paris and the one-way flights to the United States.

We arrived in Chicago, Illinois, in August 1998. My parents had connected with extended family friends, the Camtos, a Cameroonian family in Chicago. Dad had been told that they were extremely successful and ran multiple businesses. My parents saw their business savvy as an opportunity to learn from them on our next steps in the U.S.

Mr. Camtos came to pick us up at the airport in a cab—not a limousine as my siblings and I had imagined. Unknown to my family, he was a cab driver. The day of arrival was a sunny day in Chicago, and we arrived late afternoon. The drive to their house was so long I actually fell asleep. I later learned they lived on the South Side of Chicago.

I woke up when we arrived, so I did not get to see what our new neighborhood looked like. The Camtos were renting a two-bedroom, 1-bath apartment with their two sons, who were close in age to my siblings and me. They had graciously agreed to let us stay in one of the bedrooms while they stayed in the other.

My parents knew we were not happy. In Air-Bel, we stayed in a three-bedroom apartment. Our rooms had toys, and we had a TV in our living room. Now we were crammed in one room without access to the television in the living room. My parents told us to leave the room only to use the restroom so we would not disturb the family. This living situation was not what we had all hoped for, but our parents reassured us that it would be temporary. Once they had jobs, we could move out. The Camtos had agreed to let us stay in their apartment until we could settle independently.

Mr. Camtos took my dad aside the next day to share with him what he thought would be best for him to do to get started in Chicago. "Get a cab so you can start working immediately."

To Mr. Camtos's surprise, Dad said, "I have never driven a car in my life and do not have a driver's license."

My father had always been terrified of driving, so the idea of driving a cab was definitely not part of his plans. Mr. Camtos had hoped that Dad would be able to get on his feet fairly quickly, but he soon realized that my parents' acclimating to America would take time. My parents did not learn English growing up, and even though they had expended time and effort over the past year to learn the language, they had not yet reached a level where they could independently adapt to living in the States.

After staying three days with the Camtos, reality kicked in for all of us.   Mr. Camtos told my parents that we had to go somewhere else as he could no longer accommodate us. Their apartment was way too small for both families, and we knew that we were inconveniencing them. But we had no other options. My parents had been terribly misinformed about that family's ability to help us. They did not own a big house, nor did they have multiple successful businesses. Mr. Camtos was struggling to make ends meet and had so many responsibilities of his own. Many families living on Chicago's South Side faced this same reality. The area had faced significant economic challenges, including high poverty rates and a lack of quality jobs. We were left to wonder whether the South Side of Chicago was merely a replica of Air-Bel.

I recall the terror in my parents' eyes and the absolute disappointment.

They probably wondered if all the stories of successful African families in America were lies. Would they struggle again as they had in France? Was this move all for nothing? They were in a country where they could barely express themselves, and we did not have much money left from the loan they had taken to move to the United States. Mr. Camtos gave us a day to find a solution concerning our housing. They called a couple of their friends to assist us and allowed us to use their phones to call people for help. Thank God someone heard our story and connected with my parents.

Mrs. Cheny, a retired nurse, was a very kind, older Haitian woman who also spoke French. She owned a home on Chicago's South Side and lived there with her son. She agreed to let us stay in her house for a minimal fee, bringing us propitious relief. When we arrived at her house, she welcomed us with so much love into her home. She became like a grandmother to us. She had dark curly hair and wore oversized glasses. She loved makeup and jewelry and drove a bright-red car.

We were all fascinated by her house, and we felt like she was living the American Dream my parents had heard about. We were all so excited. She then took us to her basement and said, "This is where you will be staying." Though her basement looked quite dark, it was well organized with two bedrooms. My siblings and I would share the large bedroom, and my parents would stay in the smaller room. Mrs. Cheny also had a big yard, which she told us we could access anytime to play outside. I was happy because there was a TV in our living room, and I could have my playground for the first time. Even though my mom was grateful we had a home, she did not like the idea of our staying in a basement. My parents promised we wouldn't be there for long, and we had to be patient and enduring. We were just thankful we did not end up homeless.

My parents started looking for a school in which to enroll us as we had arrived only a couple of weeks from school's resuming its fall semester. For a while, my parents had in mind to enroll us in private schools, where they felt the quality of education was much better. Those in France were known to provide a high-quality education and were highly regarded by many families. My mother had always dreamed of our attending private schools. She was convinced that a high-quality education would be our greatest chance of beating the odds. However, since neither of my parents had secured employment, they knew their only option was to enroll us in a public school close to the house until they could save to afford a private school.

They began inquiring about schools in our area and quickly learned the staggering statistics surrounding the Chicago public schools. In the late 1990s, public schools on the South Side were generally characterized by gang violence and inadequate funding, which resulted in low student achievement, high dropout rates, and limited educational opportunities.

My parents had also begun to notice gang activity around our neighborhood. They saw teenagers hanging around street corners smoking and selling drugs. Our neighborhood had a significant Black population, and my parents had also noticed that most of those delinquents hanging around on the street corners were Black. My parents were ill at ease because they also had Black children and were concerned that delinquency would eventually be our fate.

Television often featured our neighborhood for high crime rates. At times, crime would occur only blocks from where we lived, which terrified my parents. Mom felt that our environment and the school we would eventually attend would be worse than Air-Bel and the schools there. She feared that we might be influenced to befriend delinquent children in school. She had not seen this level of delinquency even in Air-Bel, which had never been featured on television. She became increasingly uneasy about our living on the South Side; however, my parents had no other choice until they could stabilize financially.

We eventually enrolled in a public school ten minutes away from our house. A school bus picked us up every morning and dropped us back home in the afternoon. I found that all the students in my new school were Black. My previous school in Air-Bel was more diverse. Early on I wondered why only Black people attended this school. I saw only Black people in our neighborhood. *Where are all the other people?*

I had seen white people when we visited downtown Chicago. My family was unsure about what seemed to be a racial divide in Chicago. We were not yet familiar with the history of the city. One evening Mrs. Cheny sat down with my family to answer our questions about race and gave us a quick summary of the history of the South Side.

"Most African Americans who owned homes on our streets were middle-class families, but still, a significant portion of people still struggle in this community. I do not think this neighborhood is ideal for raising children. Sadly, my husband was murdered in our home by a burglar, and one of my own sons has become very delinquent. I did not want to share this earlier to avoid scaring you away. Please be patient and save money so you can move elsewhere in the future."

We were all in complete terror of what happened to Mr. Cheny in that same house we were living. The South Side became increasingly horrifying to my parents. To them, this area was far worse than what they were running from.

My parents eventually found work at O'Hare Airport for a food distribution company. They packaged the food people would eat on the plane. The airport was two hours away from the house by public transport. They had to take a bus and two trains to get to the airport. They also enrolled in classes at a local community college to learn English as a second language. Their schedule became exceedingly busy, with extremely long and tiring commutes. Mom worked the day shift and Dad worked the night shift. When they came home, they were exhausted. We did not spend much time with them, but we were already used to that reality in Marseille. Mom was especially unhappy about the routine we had developed in Chicago, and I saw unhappiness written on her face. In her eyes, our lives were worse now than when we had lived in France.

Contrary to how my mom felt, I enjoyed the city. My parents had taken us a couple of times to visit downtown Chicago. I saw the beautiful skyscrapers and the big cars, and I liked American food, especially the McDonald's by our house. I wanted to work in that tall skyscraper I had seen on television. I also wanted to own my home and car like I saw other Black families on our streets.

I recall discussing these possibilities with Mrs. Cheny one day, and she said, "Sonya, if you earn good grades in school, you will be able to enroll in a good university and be successful in America. You need to be serious about your future and more obedient to your parents."

In Marseille, I had developed some rebellious tendencies, but such was not the case in Chicago. We actually lived a structured life while staying with Mrs. Cheny. She encouraged us to do our homework and kept us from straying far from the house. She would often watch over us when my parents were not at home. I enjoyed her company, and I felt like she was my grandma.

In school, I was performing above average, but my family quickly noticed that our school's education level was well below average. What I was learning in subjects such as mathematics and science I had already studied in a grade lower in France. Our only challenge in school was learning English and American History, but we all quickly adjusted.

As Mom became increasingly frustrated with our school's level of academics, she became concerned that we would eventually fall behind because of attending a sub-par school. She knew our top grades meant nothing if we were not receiving a proper education. We also informed our parents of issues we noticed, including students fighting with teachers and causing chaos at school. One time the police actually showed up at the school to check out a rumor that a student had brought a gun to school. This incident raised a major red flag for my parents. My parents desperately wanted to protect us from violence.

My parents decided to seek counsel in the community colleges they were attending to assess if they could find work based on their earned university degrees. They assumed such jobs would pay much more than the minimum wage they were earning per hour. My parents met with different advisors to determine what career prospects they might have with their earned degrees. They were told they would need to start from scratch, given the language barrier and the fact that their degrees came from another country with different approaches and educational systems. This counsel displeased and greatly troubled Mom. She could not fathom starting from scratch, especially feeling that she had already sacrificed so much in France.

I often heard Mom share her discontent with my dad and that she would prefer it if we all returned to France. Mom had already done the math. She counted the years it would take them to go to school to eventually find a decent job in Chicago, as well as the cost of living and enrolling us in private schools, which were extremely expensive compared to France. Private schools in France were often part of a more extensive network of Catholic schools, which could receive government funding and have more affordable tuition.

In Mom's eyes, we would be stuck in the South Side of Chicago until she and Dad graduated...again! That length of time seemed far too long compared to staying in France. She was concerned that we would be exposed to evil influences in a poor-quality school, and the criminality in our neighborhood continued to terrify her. The math did not add up. Her dreams of a better quality of education with more excellent opportunities for us could eventually become nightmares. Well, it almost did!

My mom had taken my sister and me to have her nails done at one of the local nail shops near 79th and Jeffery. We did not go there often, but when Mom went, she often got a manicure and pedicure. That day the line was long, so we had to wait before they could attend to Mom. Because of the long wait, we left the nail salon after dark. We walked to the corner bus stop to wait for our bus to arrive. After the ten-minute bus ride, we had to walk ten more minutes to Mrs. Cheny's house. I still remember that day like yesterday.

We were seated at the bus stop, and quite a few people were also waiting. We usually enjoyed sitting down on the bus rather than standing up, so we always tried to be at the front of those waiting. As the bus slowed for our stop, we stood to be first on the bus.

Suddenly, I heard people screaming, and I immediately turned around. My worst nightmare was coming true right in front of me. A young man was trying to steal Mom's purse, which she was holding tightly. He was dragging and punching her so she would release the bag. Within seconds, I jumped into the fray to save my mom. All I could remember was screaming and grabbing the man's arm so he would stop hitting Mom. I honestly felt that an angel helped me push that man away because he let go of my mom and ran as soon as I touched him.

I always knew my mom was strong, but that day I knew she was made of steel. She was barely injured and told us she had covered her face, so she was only struck on her arm and hand. One of her nails was broken. The bus waited for us as we all made sure Mom was okay. The bus driver asked if we should call the police, but Mom insisted she was fine. The young man had already run away, and we could not identify him since he wore a face mask.

Mom's only thought was to get home quickly since she had us with her and did not want to linger outside any longer. We boarded the bus, and people willingly gave up their seats for us. Everyone stared at Mom in amazement that she had survived an attack with barely a scratch. The bus driver eventually called the police, but we did not wait for them to arrive; he remained on the phone to describe what had happened.

That incident was the final straw for Mom; that physical attack was her sign that the United States was not for her. My mother, siblings, and I returned to France in June 1999. My dad stayed in Chicago to support us financially until we were settled back in France.

Mom did not want to return to the "hole," as she often referred to Air-Bel. My parents decided that we would move to Paris, the capital of France, which boasted more economic opportunities and private schools than Marseille. Paris also had a greater concentration of businesses, financial institutions, and professional networks to offer our family more financial opportunities. We also had extended family and acquaintances living in Paris who could guide us in settling.

Well, history seemingly repeated itself. The tides seemingly kept turning against us.Upon arriving in Paris, we stayed with different family friends for couple months but eventually had to find a permanent housing solution.

Mom had used most of my parents' savings over the past couple of months. My parents were also repaying the loan for our family to move to the United States. Life in Paris was also much more expensive than in Marseille.

Mom did not tell us that we had nowhere to stay that night and could not return to that family's house. At seven o'clock in the evening, it was getting dark outside when we finally realized that Mom was searching for a place for us to sleep. She had stopped at a phone booth to call Dad, and when we heard their conversation, we knew we were in trouble.

Thankfully, Mom had collected the numbers of social assistance organizations. Only one of them picked up the phone. They immediately intervened when she told them she had children with her. The organization booked a small hotel in Creteil where we stayed for a couple of weeks. A social worker was in constant contact with Mom, putting her on the public housing waitlist in Creteil. Mom was awaiting a phone call telling us when we could finally settle into our place. She had picked up a part-time cleaning job at a luxury hotel in Paris to start saving again. Shortly before school resumed, the social worker told her they had found us a one-bedroom apartment in L'abbaye, a small commune in Creteil, where my family permanently settled.

L'abbaye in Creteil has four identical buildings with 14 floors each. These public housing buildings were very similar to the ones in Air-Bel. L'abbaye shared the same challenges and statistics as Air-Bel being a low-income environment with social and economic issues.

I intensely hated the elevators in L'abbaye, which were constantly filled with urine. We could on conclude that people high on drugs must have thought the elevator was a bathroom! We lived on the fifth floor and had no choice but to take the elevator every day with its nauseating odor.

Drug dealers had a place at the entrance of each of the four buildings, and we constantly smelled marijuana in our staircases. Over the years, we became accustomed to the habitual problem. However, in contrast to Marseille, my mom saw many more opportunities in Paris for our family to climb the economic ladder. This time my mom had a grand plan she was determined to make work.

Upon settling in Creteil, Mom met with a banker to assess what it would take financially for her to own her own home eventually. She wanted to ensure she had the financial knowledge to reach that goal. That banker gave my mom all the guidance she needed and opened multiple savings accounts for her. She also discussed with the banker her plans to enroll us in a private school, and they mapped out a financial plan for

Mom to determine how much revenue she would need. Mom decided to work two full-time jobs—one during the day as a cleaning lady in a luxury hotel, where she earned more than minimum wage, and one at night as a caretaker in a nursing home. The income she would receive, in addition to what my father would send her, would be sufficient to execute the financial plan she had worked on with the banker.

In one year, my parents would have saved enough to enroll all three of us in a private school while continuing to save. In five more years, they would have a large enough down payment to buy our family home.My mom was not a fan of public housing, but she knew she had to balance her goal of complete financial independence with the reality she was facing. Her plan gave her a sense of pride that her life was not in the hands of any system. She and her children would not end up becoming bad statistics. Unsurprisingly, my mother's plan would require her to make a tremendous sacrifice regarding sleep and the time she could spend with us. She was willing and determined to sacrifice all for us to have better economic opportunities.

At Creteil, we attended a public middle school, LaMartre, only five minutes from L'abbaye. LaMartre was known for teachers always being on strike due to students' delinquency and their insulting behavior. The teachers would often quit their job. Mom noticed the high delinquency rate in the neighborhoods where we had lived. We were once again living the same story we had lived in Air-Bel and Chicago's South Side!

Police would often visit LaMartre as students would physically fight, and school authorities needed to intervene. I had seen students fighting multiple times to the point where they would pass out. At Air-Bel, I had grown accustomed to seeing students fight in school, and I had also been a victim of a fight. Unfortunately, violence was attached to the neighborhoods where we lived. My family had become familiar with the vicious patterns in children we had noticed in low-income environments like L'Abbaye. Mom was so determined for us to beat these odds, and what we were experiencing at LaMartre was confirmation of the need for us to attend a private school with far more structure for students.

Finding a private school that would accept us was difficult. Mom was considering either private Catholic schools in Creteil or Paris. The one private school in Creteil did not admit us, and most private schools in Paris rejected our application. One day, Mom was becoming so desperate that she took us in person to visit some of those schools. Maybe she thought they would pity us, seeing that she was a desperate mother running away from the odds set against her children at L'abbaye.

The issue these schools had with our applications was that even though our grades seemed reasonable, we had attended lower-rated schools all our lives, whereas many of the other candidates had attended more competitive schools. We were competing for spots with students who had attended or transferred from top-notch private schools. One of the schools made us take an entrance exam, and my sister was the only one who barely met the qualification to enter the school. We were battling the limited space available and high academic standards.

Mom refused to give up, continuing to apply until one particular school reached out to her. This private Catholic school was located in the twelfth *arrondissement* of Paris. Our applications interested the school principal, and she asked my mom to come with us to meet her. This very short and beautiful white lady named Madame Boulard had short brown hair with red highlights and was tanned like she spent her time in the sun. She had the most beautiful brown eyes with long lashes and a welcoming smile. She immediately connected with my mom from the moment she saw her.

Mom's story touched her heart, and even though we barely met the qualifications for admission, she wanted to give us a chance. She believed our experience having lived in the United States would enrich the classroom for all students. She also somehow believed in Mom and wanted to support her vision for her children's future. Upon meeting with her, she told my mom that she would admit us to the school and negotiate a financial payment plan that would work for us. The only condition was that we needed to perform well in our first year so that we would not lower the standard of the school. Basically, we were admitted on probation. To us, Madame Boulard was indeed like an angel.

That day I could see the joy and relief written on Mom's face. Her dream of seeing us attend a private school and potentially break free from this generational cycle of adversity was finally coming true. Still, the fight was not over; it was only beginning. My parents would need to make substantial sacrifice to ensure that they maintained the plan they had set. On our end, my siblings and I needed to rise to the occasion with good grades in our classes. My family was determined to beat the odds!

Chapter 4

Struggling to Find Me in Two Different Worlds

Paris is encircled by a highway autoroute, which marks a break between the city and adjacent areas, called "Boulevard Périphérique." Paris is split into 20 arrondissements that spiral outward from the center of Paris until they reach the Boulevard Périphérique. I became familiar with commuting to Paris from L'abbaye when I started attending St. Peter private school in downtown Paris.

St. Peter was precisely 40 minutes from my house door to door—if I caught the bus going to the train station on time instead of walking. Creteil had only Train Line 8 that went straight to my school from the "Creteil Prefecture" station stop, where I caught the train. Train Line 8's route around Paris ended at "Balard," the final terminal on the other end of Paris. Our school was in the middle of the train line at "Ledru-Rollin." My siblings and I were among the very few in my school who commuted that far to school.

Every weekday, we would wake up around six o'clock in the morning to get ready, then run down the stairs of our building, and catch the bus to the station. We always ran because time was never our friend. Waking early enough to take turns in the bathroom and getting ready was difficult. Our school had a strict policy concerning lateness, and bus or train delays were not acceptable excuses. Students had no more than three strikes before teachers would report tardiness in our report card. My siblings and I became used to having tardiness noted on our report cards.

I will never forget my first journey to St. Peter as a student. The day was fascinating. We had heard Mom speak about private school for years, and we had an inaccurate image in our minds that attending a private school would somehow solve all our problems. Going to a private school made me feel like we had risen in society and technically, we were no longer struggling. We all woke up very early on that first day of going to St. Peter. Mom had bought us new clothes, school bags, and school items. I felt like we had a fresh new beginning. I proudly wore my new outfit, and Mom had braided my sister's and my hair. We all wanted to make a great impression going to school. I fixed my breakfast while waiting for my siblings to get ready. I was sitting in our living room with Mom, repeatedly rehearsing the journey we would take to go to school.

We had become familiar with taking the bus and train on our own in the past, but she wanted to ensure our safe arrival. Mom had purchased our yearly transportation pass covering Zone 1 to 3, the zones we would cross to get to school. Creteil was in Zone 3, and Paris covers Zone 1 and 2. The higher numbers represented zones in faraway suburbs. The higher the zone, the higher the fee for the transportation pass. That transportation fee alone was probably one of the reasons why many of my friends in Creteil did not often visit Paris. Because we were students, the transportation pass was less expensive, but Mom had even budgeted these passes in her grand plan. She could not take us to school that day as she had to leave for work right after we departed.

Mom began encouraging me. "Sonya, I want you to focus in class. That you do not rebel against your teacher is very important. You could get expelled for that insubordination. I want you to make a great first impression." Mom wanted each one of us to be well-prepared to begin this new journey.

Mom's eyes were joyous as she saw her dreams starting to come true.

She had planned for this day for years. Skipping the elevator ride, Mom walked us down the staircase of the building when my siblings were finally ready. We did not want that terrible smell we were accustomed to in the elevator to follow us to our prestigious school. Since we had left early that morning, we did not have to run to the bus stop. We knew that we would arrive at school on time. The bus came almost immediately after we arrived at the bus stop.

The weather in the early fall was usually cloudy, but it did not rain that day. When we got to the train station, we saw the train was about to arrive from afar, so we quickly passed through the entrance point and rushed down the stairs to catch the train. Though the train followed a regular schedule, at times the strikes in France made the schedule unreliable. We also wanted to ensure we had good seats since the train ride to our school would be long. We usually had great seats since our train stop was the first one, but it could get crowded at that time of the day. Fortunately, we arrived on time to all have window seats on the train.

We had taken that same train in the past to visit Paris with Mom, but that journey felt different. We did not talk while on the train; we stared out the window as the train carried us from stop to stop. We clearly noticed while commuting to school how the demographics changed the closer we got to Paris. We saw more Black people at our train stop, but the closer we got to Paris, we would see more white people. We soon became used to this reality of commuting.

When we arrived at our stop, we noticed other students who had taken the train to get to school. We were all a little anxious about making new friends, so we did not look at any students or smile at them. As Mom had shown us, we simply walked straight to school, which was located on a very narrow street and was surrounded by residential buildings. That area of Paris was very crowded as our school was very close to major

Parisian attractions. A McDonald's restaurant was located at the exit of the train as were smaller shops as we walked toward the school. Right beside the school was a boulangerie, where students would often go for their snacks.

On that day, many students were waiting with their parents at the school's main entrance for middle and high school students. The school had a separate entrance for elementary school students. When my siblings and I entered the school's main entrance, we had to push through a massive double door made of wood. Security personnel then checked whether our names were on the student roster before letting us in. Once we passed security, we opened another double glass door, which led straight to the schoolground play area at the center of the school. That playground, which was surrounded by the school building, was not big, so I felt very confined there that day.

Many students were trying to figure out where their classes were. Teachers were standing at distinctive pillars of the school playground, and on each pillar was a paper with a class level and the names of the students in that class. My siblings and I separated since we were all in different grades. I was in one of the three seventh grade classes, so I went to the proper pillar.

I recall reading the names of the other students that day. I was curious to see who would soon become my friends. What immediately caught my attention was that many of these students had French names. I thought they were most likely pure *souche*, referring to people with French ancestry, without any immigrant heritage. Pure souche could usually be distinguished by their last names that were common French names.

At Air-Bel and L'abbaye, I was used to seeing most of my classmates' last names being of immigrant heritage. Such was not the case at St Peter. When the time came to start heading to class, our teacher asked us to form a line and walk together to our class. My class was on the third floor of the left building where middle school classes were held. As I sat in my class, I soon realized that only two out of the twenty-five students in that class were Black students. My sister and brother were the only Black kids in their classes. That realization initially intimidated me, but I did not let the disparity get to me.

We had different teachers based on the class subject. I soon discovered our history teacher had walked us to class that morning. We also had French, math, and science classes that same day. Each teacher asked us to introduce ourselves at the beginning of the class by stating our names and whether we were new or returning to the school.

Every time the teachers came to me, they would often pause because my last name, "Mbatchou," appeared complicated for them to say. "Sonya, how do I say your last name? Do I pronounce the 'M'?"

"No, the 'M' is silent. I am new to this school," I added.

"What school did you attend last year?"

Because of this series of questions and answers in each class, everyone now knew that my siblings and I were commuting to school from Creteil.

The school scheduled two breaks during the day—one in the morning for 15 minutes, and one during lunchtime for 45 minutes. During those breaks, I introduced myself to my classmates and immediately bonded with the other Black girl in my class. We eventually sat next to each other in class. Some students already knew each other from the previous year, but about half were new students.

I felt a great connection with most of my classmates, which gave me a great impression of the school. During school lunch, Mom had given us pocket money to eat outside that day. The plan was for us to take food from home and warm it in school, but she wanted to make our first day of school special. I ate at the local McDonald's with some new classmates that day. School ended every day for the most part around four o'clock in the afternoon.

I met my siblings at the entrance when school was over so we could return home together. I realized some classmates also had to take the train back home. Most of them lived in Paris, and only one of my classmates lived in the banlieue like me. On the train, I shared with my siblings what had happened that day and who I had met. My siblings also had a great time in school and felt good about this new school environment. When we got home, we were exhausted from the commute and the thrill of the day.

Mom was scheduled to work that evening and was about to leave when we arrived home. Excitedly, she greeted us and asked how our first day went. We all had great stories to share. I told her we were among the very few Black people in the school. "Do you feel out of place?" she asked, but we told her that we had felt very welcomed by everyone. She was relieved that we had been accepted at the school, and she had such sense of peace, knowing she had made the right decision. Going to St. Peter became part of my weekday routine for six years until I graduated from high school.

I loved going to school in Paris. The beauty I saw in Paris made the daily commute enjoyable. The architecture of the buildings was very different than what I was used to in Creteil. The buildings and monuments in Paris are a fascinating blend of various styles and influences, which reflects Paris's rich history and cultural heritage. From the moment I got off at the Ledru-Rollin train stop, I was surrounded by Haussmanian architecture. Symmetrical facades, large windows with small balconies, with cream-colored stones on the exteriors characterized these buildings. In my eyes, the eloquence of Parisian architecture signified prestige.

Going to school in Paris made me forget how much I had come to hate public housing and the horrific odors I associated with my building. I could be proud of my exquisite school. My school gave me an identity

"Going to school in Paris made me forget how much I had come to hate public housing and the horrific odors I associated with my building."

that lifted me above poverty and shame.

Many of my friends lived in beautiful properties, and they would often invite me to have lunch with them. Most of them lived in beautiful homes not far from the school. I was amazed at how their houses were structured and how welcoming they made me feel. I often would tell my classmates in amazement how fortunate they were to have their own room. However, I noticed that what they had was not something that seemed particularly special to them.

After a while, most of my classmates stopped inviting me because I was somehow expected to return the favor. "If I invite you for lunch, you must eventually invite me too." Imagine the shock I felt when a classmate asked me for the first time if she could visit me in Creteil. The thought was terrifying, and I had to cook a lie for them to leave me alone. *I could never invite my classmates to my home*, my mind screamed.

In fact, with time, I started becoming extremely ashamed of my family's living conditions. The idea of my classmates seeing that I lived in one of those tall, dirty, public-housing buildings terrified me. I did not want to be the outcast, even though I often felt like it at St. Peter. I wanted to develop an identity away from home, but reality would kick back every time I stepped back into L'abbaye. With time, I almost became taboo among my classmates simply because I had never invited them to my home. However, I did not care. To forge excuses sounded better than ever having to invite them home, so I never did. I never once invited anyone to L'abbaye.

I started developing a low self-esteem problem after enrolling at St. Peter. My circumstances made me ashamed of myself, and constantly comparing myself to my classmates did not help. I always felt that they had this perfect life filled with comfort and that my family, on the contrary, lived a shameful life. These feelings aided in creating a sense of isolation as I started seeing my world at St. Peter as me versus them. I internalized those emotions—never expressing them to anyone.

A deep resentment toward my mom began building. I felt that she was the one to blame for the fact that we were struggling. At that time in my teenage life, I started arguing with her at home. I could not understand why she always worked but never had any money. When my friends planned to go to a movie or to a restaurant for lunch, I could not join them because I did not have the money. Mom was teaching me contentment, but that intangible response was not something my teenage self could understand. I always felt like I was missing out on life.

———————

Anna was one of the close friends I made in ninth grade. Her parents were pharmacists, and she sometimes invited me to hang out at her house over the weekend. She lived in a three-bedroom condo building in the center of Paris. I remember her parents laughing the first time they met me because of my amazement at their beautiful home. One particular Saturday, Anna wanted to go shopping, and her mom agreed to take us. As Anna and I were getting ready in her room, she let me use some of her makeup. We pretended to be models while staring in the large mirror in her room. Anna's mom called her on her cell phone to come down as she had arrived in front of the house with the car. We rushed down the stairs, and I saw...

Anna's family owned a beautiful black Mercedez-Benz! I couldn't believe we would be riding in that car all afternoon. I truly felt like a celebrity that day. Her mom drove us to Belleville, a neighborhood in the twentieth arrondissement of Paris filled with vintage stores. Anna's mom thought Belleville would be an excellent spot with an abundance of affordable clothing, She knew that we only had a small budget. I had come with 10 euros, which was all my mother could give me. I had argued with my mom all morning that day because I felt what she had given me was insufficient for shopping.

Mom would not have it. She had recognized that I often played the comparison game. "You need to be content with your lifestyle! Be patient and stop comparing yourself to your classmates."

In all my criticism of her, I would tell her that other parents were better than she was. Anna's mom was great because she had given her daughter 200 euros to go shopping.

Anna's mom dropped us off at one of the stores and told us she would circle before picking us up later. We jumped from the car and started going from store to store. To my disappointment, I bought only one shirt that day, while Anne purchased a bag full of clothes. I was envious of my friend and filled with resentment toward my mom. When we ended shopping that day, Anna's mom dropped me at the nearest train station, Line 8, which went straight to my home in Creteil.

I cried on my way back home that day. I could not understand why I was missing out on many things I felt my classmates had. I embraced that sentiment most of my time at St. Peter. *What is wrong with my family? Why do I feel so much shame attached to my life?*

I felt such a huge sense of inadequacy, and I believed people like me were not fortunate to live a life of privilege. Life was hard, and the comparison game started creating a bridge between Mom and me.

Teenagers go through this phase of trying to define who they are, separate from their parents. I started to define myself through my environment, unconsciously carrying the negative identity of L'abbaye— if I lived in such deprived conditions, I was not worthy. I constantly compared my life at l'Abbaye to how my classmates in Paris lived and nursed a constant feeling of being inadequate. As much as I loved attending St. Peter, my reality created an internal struggle of being constantly ashamed of my family and me. I lived in two worlds between L'abbaye and Paris, and I wanted to understand where I was supposed to fit in.

In the mix of all this soul-searching, the home front added more issues. Years of unachieved dreams and constant struggle significantly impacted my parents' marriage. Both had developed different visions for life. Mom had been terrified at the prospect of our future in Chicago, convinced that we would have better future outcomes in France. On the other hand, Dad believed in the American dream as France did not deliver the hopes he so desperately had. He no longer planned on permanently joining us in France.

Over the years, my parents argued tremendously over this matter. Their constant arguing eventually separated them, affecting our family—especially me. The impact of their issues, coupled with my search for my own identity amid differences I saw in my worlds, caused me to develop an aggressive nature. These issues revived the rebellious tendencies I had left behind in Air-Bel. I had come to hate being home. As a teenager, I felt trapped in that small one-bedroom apartment, embarrassed at the life my family was living, and hearing constant arguing with nowhere to run.

I would constantly argue with my mom. Was it the daily smell of urine in the elevators that so often reminded me that we were stuck in this cycle of shame? I had no one to whom I could express those feelings, and being away from home was a way to cope easily with what was happening in my family. I felt like I was back in Air-Bel, where I disliked being home because my mom was never there, and if she was, we would often argue. My internal coping mechanism for a challenge was always to run away from home.

With my rebellious nature in full bloom, I started associating with the wrong crowd at L'abbaye. Over the years at L'abbaye, I became friends with some of my teenage neighbors, who reminded me of the friends I had at Air-Bel. The majority of the demographics of people living at

L'abbaye were of African descent. France does not include data in its census on race and ethnicity, but from what I saw over the years of living at L'abbaye, a specific demographic of people was centralized there.

I met Drame and Sofia while attending a familiar friend's birthday party in L'abbaye. In France, asking people about their origins was customary. I learned Drame was originally from Mali, and Sofia was of Moroccan descent. Even if they were born in France, people were always curious about another's roots.

Drame and Sofia were already close friends when I met them as they attended LaMartre together. Sofia lived in a building right behind L'abbaye, and I could see her apartment from my window. When I met Drame and Sofia, I was immediately reminded of my friendship with Sonia in Marseille and the common struggle we shared. Sofia had a booming voice as I did, and she loved to laugh very loud. Drame and Sofia loved being away from home, hating the restrictions they faced when home.

They both resented their parents' traditional lifestyle, and their parents barely allowed them to go outside. I could relate to their feeling of not wanting to stay at home. In Drame's family, the women tended to marry once they turned 16. They were told that women should stay home with their mothers, where they would learn to cook and prepare for marriage. Sofia's dad had already spoken to her about marriage after graduating high school.

I could relate to their struggle. Just like Drame and Sofia, I wanted to run away from my home life. We all harbored a lot of internal emotions we wanted to repress, and running away was the best way we could think of. We felt free from what we resented whenever we were away from home. Through Drame and Sofia, I started connecting with a new group of friends and became increasingly rebellious. We were like a clique of teenagers in search of our identity away from home. To us, *home* signified shame, trouble, and struggles.

We were always looking for opportunities to go out. This group of friends was very different from those I had previously made at L'abbaye like Drea or my friends at St. Peter. Outward displays of rebellion characterized them. With them, I started yelling at people publicly and cursing—using language never condoned in my family or at St Peter. They would consistently fight with their parents and teachers. I knew that behavior would not be tolerated at St. Peter. Yet, with time, I became used to my friends' misbehavior and started enjoying the rebellious activities we would do together as our way of expressing the anger we had internalized.

We became obsessed with one common topic: whether French society was racist against people like us. I knew social challenges played out in communities like L'abbaye with its sizeable African-immigrant population. However, I was always conflicted about whether those challenges were indeed "racism." The truth was that I never felt that I experienced racism. In school, even though I was one of the few Black people attending, I always felt that being a person of color had made me stand out as opposed to pushing me down. I usually felt initially uncomfortable in a crowd of people where I was the only Black person, but with time, I had gotten used to it. My teachers had always been interested in my success, and I always felt like a favorite to some of them. I also enjoyed interacting with classmates at school and never felt they discriminated against me. However, the more time I spent with my neighborhood friends, the more I started accepting the same beliefs they had that "our families' struggles were due to being denied opportunities contrary to how *white* people were treated in France".

The media also portrayed the stigma of "at-risk" youth living in neighborhoods like L'abbaye. The high delinquency rate and criminality found in certain cité like L'abbaye scared many people, including the police. On television, mainly youth of African descent were shown as delinquents or criminals. So, an apparent resentment started to build among us toward white French people and what we thought was some form of "white privilege."

With time, we started justifying our delinquent behavior with what we thought was a fight against the injustice we faced in France. We started doing outside of our homes whatever we wanted to do without any restrictions as our way to express our resentment for the struggles our families were experiencing and the resulting shame we had long felt. We were rebelling against French society for putting our families and us in what we felt was a shameful pit. We had the right to act however we wanted because we were disadvantaged and discriminated against. At least, that is what we thought.

I recall a scene that took place one day when we took the RER, a fast train passing through Paris and its surrounding suburbs. We caught the RER to Aulnay-sous-bois to go to a party. Mom had no idea I would leave the house to go that far. She always thought I would stay around L'abbaye, or at the farthest go to the mall—unless I was hanging out in Paris with my classmates.

Aulnay-sous-bois, a banlieue located in the Seine-Saint-Denis department, was over an hour from our house. This neighborhood had a very negative reputation due to many delinquent activities. Contrary to L'abbaye, Aulnay-sous-Bois was constantly featured on television news. My mom would have been terrified if she knew it was where I had gone that day with my clique. On our way to Aulnay-sous-bois that Saturday, I soon realized that my train pass did not cover Zone 4.

Most of my friends with me that day also did not have a pass to cover that zone, so we all jumped the gate without paying. I was terrified of getting caught, but we didn't that day. On the train, we were all very loud. One of the guys with us, Ahmed, was playing loud music. We even screamed our views on the train of how racist the French society was.

We could tell people were very annoyed at our behavior, but we convinced ourselves that their indignation was because they were racists. I was secretly embarrassed by what we were doing on the train, but I did not say anything because I wanted to fit in. What scared me most was that my classmates and their parents would see me doing what we were doing. I was terrified that my St. Peter classmates would learn about the "other life" I was living at L'abbaye. Nevertheless, I followed the crowd to that party and we stayed there until two o'clock in the morning.

At that party, Ahmed introduced Betsie and Kendra to me, who were already close friends. I don't think I knew until about midnight that the last train to take me back home had already left. Since it was a Sunday, the next train to get home would not come until five o'clock in the morning. When I talked to Betsie about train schedule, she laughed uncontrollably at the fear in my eyes. I knew Mom would get home before me and know that I had not spent the night at home.

Betsie thought staying out all night was cool, but we had nowhere to stay that evening. After all, none of us lived in the area. Even Betsie and Kendra had commuted from a distant cité to get there. The night was dark, and I had no idea how to return to the train station. Only Ahmed seemed to know the way back to the station. We could have at least stayed at the train station until the next train came. Unfortunately, that night was freezing, and the train station was closed. We decided to return to the building where the party was, and we sat inside on one of the staircases. We felt warmer there even though we were very uncomfortable.

I did not fall asleep that early morning. I kept thinking of my mom, who I knew would be terribly upset with me. I began rehearsing words I would use to argue with her. As much as I thought being with my friends was fun, a constant feeling of unease within me told me that what we were doing was terribly wrong. What I did with these neighborhood friends was not something I would ever discuss at school. But I was living a double life..

Mom was furious when I got home. I think she yelled at me that entire day. We argued back and forth the entire time. I knew Mom was working so hard to give us a life she never had, and she was terrified at the idea of my destroying her plans. During that rebellious phase, my teenage mind simply did not get it. Mom did not like my friendship with Drame and Sofia, believing they meant trouble and were no good for me from the first day they had knocked at the door. I felt like my new friends understood me while she didn't.

Our relationship was a constant back-and-forth argument. Mom was quite concerned that this new group of friends would impact my behavior and grades in school. I spent most of my evenings and weekend with them instead of doing my homework, so she knew my grades would eventually plummet. Unfortunately, most of my interactions with Mom only made me angrier at her for feeling that she could not understand me instead of seeing that she cared deeply about me and my future. I kept returning to my clique, despising her warnings and reprimands.

My behavior at school did begin to change. The influence of this circle of friends was beginning to show. These friends also struggled in school, and half had dropped out of high school. By the time I reached tenth grade, my rebellion at school had reached an all-time high. My neighborhood friends had successfully influenced my behavior to begin doing what I had once called shameful. I started yelling back at my teachers and fighting with my classmates. I began cursing with no filter. I became the very image of stigmatized Black youth as publicized by the media.

I was now the delinquent Black girl in school. Some of my classmates started calling me *racaille* (thug), the term coined for delinquent youth living in places like L'abbaye. Some of my teachers, who had known me for years, initially thought I was passing through a teenage phase. They would instruct me to change my behavior so that it would not negatively impact me. They knew I was not that racaille described on television, but I failed to yield to their counsel.

I was one of two students nominated by my classmates as the class lead—a person who was supposed to lead the class by example, organize events for students, and attend quarterly teachers' meetings to review students' performance. It was the month of May, and we were about to wrap up tenth grade. The class leads would be present at the upcoming teachers' meeting, and teachers would individually review each student's performance. When teachers would discuss the performance of a class lead, that student would step outside the room.

I remember sitting down in that particular teachers' meeting and seeing the summary performance of every student in my class. As I looked at my name, I saw that I was the top student in my class. I had earned the highest average grade. I was excited, but I knew that most of my teachers were disappointed with my behavior in class. I had to step out to the hallway when they discussed my name. I recall that meeting being particularly long, and I could not wait to ask the other class lead what had been said.

I was smart and earned high grades but my rebellious behavior could not be overlooked. My teachers expressed concern that my behavior was changing for the worse, and they had no choice but to note it in my report card. That one negative report could impact my university admission. They had repeatedly warned me, but I was unyielding, and they were concerned that I was influencing the behavior of other students. They issued warnings in my high school report that my behavior was not indicative of my grades. Their censure made me angry, and I started interpreting my teachers' correction of me as a sign of racism.

The issue was that I needed to realize the impact of my actions and take full responsibility for them. Myself and my neighborhood clique were not taking responsibility for how badly we behaved; we thought our fight was against social injustice. Even after that teachers' meeting and my mom's scolding, I continued to display bad behavior. Each quarterly school report became increasingly more negative. I was given warning after warning, and my grades began slowly falling. I was unstoppable as I headed down a very tragic path.

To top it all off, I told my mom I wanted to quit my school and attend the local public high school in Creteil. I told her that my school had become racist toward me, and I would rather go to school with people who at least looked like me. In school, some of my teachers could no longer tolerate my behavior and my insults. When I talked in class and distracted other students or argued with professors over mundane issues, they would expelled me from their class. I took those expulsions as rejection instead of correction.

Mom was in complete despair; she no longer knew what to do. She had expressed her frustration to my dad and her family.I would not listen to them either. It came as no surprise that I eventually ended up at the police station. However, the aftermath of my being arrested brought change in my life—an answer to Mom's cries and prayers.

I met with Madame Boulard the week after she met with my mom about the police incident. Her office was on the fourth floor—the same floor as the teachers' office. Only the high school seniors who had some classes on that floor were allowed to be there. I was only a junior, my presence on that floor implied that I was in trouble—again.

I bowed my head low so no one would see me walk to the principal's office, but I knew some of the teachers saw me. *They're probably hoping that the principal will help me straighten up.* They were unaware of what had happened at the police station, and I don't believe Madame Boulard ever told them. When I arrived at her office, her door was already open. She was sitting behind her desk, smiling, and waiting for me. She asked me to come in, stood, walked to the door, and closed it behind me. I sat in fear, wondering what she had discussed with my mother and whether I was in some sort of trouble.

She began our appointment by summarizing what my mother had told her about the police incident. "Your mom wants accountability to ensure you do not return to your old ways. Your mom was very transparent about your behavior at home. I believe she is doing everything in her power to keep you in check."

I had not been expelled from school because Madame Boulard believed wholeheartedly in Mom's dream to see her children receive a good education. She had seen over the years how hard my mother had worked to provide financially for us to attend St. Peter but Madame Boulard still had to keep me in check. At that meeting, Mom told the principal what had happened, about the police officer who had spoken to me, and that I had promised him that I would no longer rebel at home or school.

Madame Boulard let me know she was shocked and disappointed to hear about what I had done, but she was also relieved to know that someone could speak sense into me. My mom also shared the comments I had made about my school's being racist and my insisting that I should attend a local school in Creteil with more Black students.

Madame Boulard had been like a loving mom to my mother. She empathized so well with my mother's challenges of working so much while raising teenagers, including a very rebellious one. Mom would always come home reassured after speaking to Madame Boulard. When Mom faced financial challenges in paying school fees, Madame Boulard often provided discounts and very lenient payment plans. Madame Boulard was like an angel sent to my mom, and she always welcomed me tenderly to her office despite the dire reports she would hear about me.

She asked me to confirm if the information Mom had shared was correct. I nodded in fear to acknowledge what she had said, and with a quiet voice, I replied, "Yes."

"Would you like to share your concerns with me about this school and racism that you have told your mom?"

Interestingly, she wanted to hear me out and what was in my mind. She did not scold me or reprimand me for my sharing my thoughts. Maybe she somehow knew I had suffered enough in that prison cell.

"I have been feeling for a while that something is wrong with my being one of the few Black people in the school. Being constantly expelled from class made me feel alienated and bullied. I do not feel that the teachers were being fair with how they treated me versus other students who also misbehaved in class. I am working on not being rebellious anymore, and I will do my best to catch up with my classes and not fail them. However, I do think I would do better in school if I attended a school with more Black people so I would not feel insecure about myself."

"Sonya, thank you for your honesty and for sharing your concerns," Madame Boulard said. "It is important for our school to take corrective actions for student misbehavior in or outside of class. Since you have decided to change for the better, I will trust you and what you have told me. But, we will keep close watch on your behavior. I am so sorry you have felt ostracized for so long. I truly believe you will one day change the narrative for the better about what is commonly said about Black youth living in a cité like yours. However, to do so, you will need to stay extremely focused. Rebelling the way you did was not the way to fight what you perceived as injustice. Instead, you need to focus on succeeding at school to become an example for others. I have no doubt in my mind that you are extremely smart, and I believe you could achieve great things if you will stay focused."

After my appointment with her, I felt peace within me because I knew she understood me and the identity challenge I was facing. She did not shame me. Her words, the police officer's words, and my mom's continuous belief in me gave me the courage to take responsibility for my actions, refocus, and get back on track in my academics.

My time had come to rise from the ashes.

Chapter 5

My Time to Rise from the Ashes

I ended my junior year with a terrible report card, so I spent the summer preparing for my senior year by catching up on classes. I was concerned that if I did not catch up, I would not be able to pass the *Baccalauréat* (BAC), a mandatory exam to matriculate to higher education institutions in France. The BAC exam is one of the most critical exams in France and is a crucial factor in determining a student's future educational and career prospects.

I was apprehensive that I would not be able to pass the BAC by the end of my senior year. To top it off, my high school report was also less than desirable due to my previous misconduct in classes. I was also concerned whether I would even have a shot at getting into a good university. In my school, many students dreamed of taking "preparatory classes" to gain admission into France's most prestigious schools, the *Grandes Écoles*, which were comparable to the Ivy Leagues in the United States. The Grande Écoles are recognized as France's best institutions of higher learning for engineering, business, and management studies.

I had once aspired to enter a Grande École to study financial engineering. Still, with my terrible behavior in school highlighted in my report card and falling grades, I knew I had a very slim chance of being accepted into any of them. I wanted to become a financial engineer trading stocks in places like Wall Street, and the best route for me to get there in France would have been attending one of the Grandes Écoles.

Seeing and understanding that I likely forfeited many great opportunities was incredibly painful. I was unsure what would be left for me.

I spent the summer feeling guilty about myself and wanted a chance at redemption so badly. My eyes had finally been opened, and I wanted to find a way to redeem myself. In the forefront of my mind was fearing that my parents' efforts would have been in vain. The only and last hope I had was to maximize my summer by trying to catch up, by doing well my senior year, and gaining my teachers' recommendation. Perhaps, I could still gain admission into one of these top schools.

One of the apparent decisions I had to make was to break off some of my destructive friendships. As much as I loved every friend in my clique, I realized that our association was toxic and in no way mutually beneficial. *Mom was right all along.* They were not *bad* people, but the fruits of what we had been doing together were wrong and destructive. The police officer had told me I could influence them for good if I would get it right. I knew partying my life away on weekends or hanging out aimlessly with them would lead us nowhere.

I had to shift my priorities and align my friendships with those who were going where I was going and focused on building a future for themselves. Mom told me to call some of my classmates with whom I once used to be close and who were very focused in class. "Schedule a time to meet them at the library over the summer. That will motivate all of you to stay focused. You can ask them questions in the areas where you have fallen behind."

I decided to follow Mom's advice, and I called Aria and Adrian. Most of my other classmates had traveled away for the summer, but Aria and Adrian were around and immediately accepted my suggestion to go to the library over the summer months.

Aria was very direct with me on that call and stated in no uncertain terms, "You will have to completely give up that "thug" life as it will not profit you! I am happy to see that you are getting serious again."

I loved how focused Aria was. She wanted to become a scientific researcher studying diseases like Parkinson's. Like my mom, her parents were hard-working immigrants from Sri Lanka who greatly valued education.

They were spending their savings putting Aria and her brother in private school. They understood that education was their opportunity to succeed in French society. Mom loved Aria and encouraged me to spend all summer with her.

Adrian was a highly ambitious French native. I believe he might well have been the most ambitious student in our class. From a very young age, his parents had drilled in him the importance of matriculating to a Grande École. His very successful father had attended a Grande École. Adrian had a clear path traced for himself, and he was more than ready to compete to get into the preparatory classes after high school. Studying was Adrian's weapon to life. He had a strong competitive nature. He loved every chance he could get to study to beat the other students. I was not surprised that Adrian was one of the top students.

Adrian's drive inspired me greatly, and in a way, I envied him. I felt Adrian had been privileged to live the life my family had always aspired to live. Adrian lived in a giant condo in a costly neighborhood of Paris. Aria and I were amazed the first day we walked into his house that most would describe as a mansion. Adrian's family was what French society considered upper class. Adrian had grown up with wealth and comfort— at least that is how I interpreted his life. Wealth and comfort were not my realities in our one-bedroom public housing apartment and being around Adrian brought these realities to life.

Aria and I enjoyed the competitive spirit Adrian brought to our study time. We knew we needed that spirit to rise in France's very competitive education system, especially for those desiring to join the most elite post-secondary schools. Adrian also agreed to join us at the library over the summer. Both Aria and Adrian lived in Paris, and we agreed to meet at the National Library of France—the François-Mitterrand Campus Library (BnF). Our meeting place was located in the thirteenth arrondissement of Paris and perfectly centered so that none of us had to travel a great distance. I had to travel the farthest—about 40 minutes from my house. Adrian and Aria each lived about 25 minutes from the BnF.

Going to the BnF library over the summer was like a journey I was taking to reach my dreams. Working with Adrian and Aria gave me new ambitions. We often discussed our future careers and what we would become in French society. Adrian's ambitions pushed both Aria and me to dream higher. The beauty and prestige of the BnF Library with its mix of modern and historical styles also made our dreams ever more palatable. Shelves filled with books reached the high ceilings of the library. The arched corners seemed to form a dome made of glass. Every time I entered the BnF, I felt one step closer to achieving my dream. I had hope after all that I would rise on top my senior year and excel in my classes. I was determined not to remain stuck in L'abbaye.

The line to enter BnF was often very long, and we would wait as long as an hour, even during the summer. We didn't mind. We would use the waiting line to discuss future career ambitions, and later on, we would use that time to memorize what we had written in our flashcards as we prepared for the BAC.

Aria and I became very close friends during that summer. Her background was very similar to mine. Her parents also had humble beginnings, and Aria also dreamt of a better life for her family. What Aria had that I so desperately needed was *focus*. She did not get distracted from her career goal. She did not let the struggles her family faced divert her. Aria also felt out of place in school. As a woman of color, she too had felt uneasy among people who looked nothing like her. In a way, that aspect of her life also contributed to our becoming closer. We knew we were defying the odds as we encouraged each other through that journey.

The closer Aria and I became, the farther away my neighborhood clique was from me. I had stopped the crazy partying and hanging out with them, and with time, we lost interest in each other. Our ambitions no longer aligned. The few friends I stayed close with at L'Abbaye, like Drea, supported me in refocusing my energy on what would benefit my future—not destroy it. I started sharing with them what I was doing with Aria and Adrian, and my newfound ambitions also motivated them to rise higher than the life we had at L'abbaye.

I had shared stories of my experiences at St. Peter with Drea. Because she was so curious about my school, I invited Drea to visit St. Peter. She was wholly fascinated about the world I was living there. After all, Drea had very little interaction with people outside of Creteil. I don't think Drea had ever visited Paris other than passing through to go to another banlieue. Years had passed since Drea had gone to Paris. She was so used to her routine and Creteil that she had no reason to go to Paris.

Drea lived in a very traditional home. She was only allowed to go to school, go out to buy groceries, visit me or family, and for the most part, she stayed home. Drea's parents were strict; as the eldest of seven, Drea was expected to be an obedient role model to her siblings. Drea's parents had moved to France from Mali. Though they had lived in France for ten years, they had only brought Drea to France after five years when she was eleven. At that time, we became friends.

Drea's father was a sanitation worker, and her mother was a stay-at-home mom. Drea's parents loved me—even after the police incident. They were inspired by what my mother was doing to give us better opportunities in France. Mom had pressed upon Drea's parents the need for them to allow her to pursue higher education beyond high school.

Mom knew that in part of their culture, the women usually married young and become stay-at-home mothers. Mom also knew that Drea aspired to do far more than that with her life; therefore, my mother wanted to advocate for her. Thankfully, her parents finally yielded to Mom's counsel. They felt that my friendship with Drea would motivate her to rise higher.

Drea's dream was to have a career that would enable her to care for her family and her parents in their old age. Drea did not imagine a life away from Creteil as I did. Everything outside of our neighborhood was so foreign and frightening to her. I showed her around the outer premises of my school that summer since the school was closed. We also walked to La Bastille, a mere ten minutes from St. Peter. She saw places in Paris she had never seen.

On our train ride home, Drea was quiet most of the way. I felt that she was most likely meditating about our day in the big city. I can only remember her telling me that I was highly blessed to have my opportunities and that she genuinely believed I would become someone great. Drea always dreamt of going to the United States one day, and she had many times encouraged me to return there when I completed high school. She mentioned again that day before we parted ways that I should consider looking for a university in Chicago.

Given that I was so focused on the BAC and giving my all to redeem my chance at getting into a Grande École, the reality of studying in the United States seemed distant. I always thought I would study first in France and then work on Wall Street. I had no idea that what Drea had in mind was in line with what my mom also wished for me.

Something tragic happened at the end of that summer. A group of teenage girls living in L'Haÿ-les-Roses, an adjacent banlieue to the one where I lived, argued with one of their friends and to retaliate, they decided to set fire to her mailbox. Something seemingly small like setting the mailbox on fire in that big public housing building culminated in starting the whole building on fire, resulting in 18 deaths by smoke inhalation.

The incident became a major news story, and everyone in our neighborhood was talking about those teenagers. The story terrified my mother because she knew it could have been me. She knew the neighborhood group with whom I would hang out could have committed a similar offense. When I got home from the library that day, that fire and how those teenage girls reminded her of me was all she talked about at home. "Any one of them could have been my daughter," she moaned. In the back of her mind, Mom was always afraid that I would go back to associating with that former clique. That news stories evoked a great deal of fear in her. *What if Sonya goes back to her old ways? What if these friends come back to knock at our door?* Mom wanted me away from our neighborhood, and she wanted a plan in place for me to get away after I graduated from high school.

Unknown to me, Mom was very proud of the changes she saw in me and decided to share some of my newfound ambitions with her siblings. "Sonya has decided to change for the better, and she is spending most of her days in the library." Of course, she also shared with her siblings the tragic news story at L'Haÿ-les-Roses and her desire for me to leave the area.

Aunty Christine had moved to the United States the year we left Chicago. Her dad had instilled in her and her siblings a passion for education. My grandfather particularly told my aunt and mother that they were geniuses and believed they had superior academic abilities. Unfortunately, my grandfather could never afford to send them to high school.Instead, they had to work early to help provide for the family.

Nevertheless, he planted a seed that made my aunt and mother dream of pursuing higher education.

Aunty Christine had opened a hair salon in Chicago's South Side and had become financially independent through that business. However, that summer as I was going into my senior year of high school, Mom told me that Aunty Christine had closed the salon to return to school. My aunt had achieved great success with her salon, and I was amazed that she was willing to start basically from scratch.

My aunt had never attended high school, but I always knew she had superior abilities in mathematics. She took courses to catch up at the university level and told my mother that she had started courses in a subject she believed would interest me. Mom had discussed with my aunt about my ambitions to become a financial engineer, and my aunt shared that she might have some career advice for me based on her research of potential careers in mathematics.

Aunty Christine called me in early September to chat with me about what careers interested me. I told her I was interested in the stock market and wanted a career combining mathematics and finance. She immediately stopped me and excitedly said, "I have the perfect career track for you! Research what an actuary is and does. I will send you some notes that explain what this career is. Actuaries have lucrative and very stable careers—contrary to being stock traders/financial engineers, which can be very volatile. Sonya, you should consider applying to the school I attend, DePaul University, to study actuarial science. During your fall break, come visit the university campus to see if that career would interest you."

I shared my concern about my report card being full of warnings due to my rebellious behavior.

"Sonya, if your performance improves during your senior year, the university will admit you," she encouraged.

I accepted her offer to visit her, check out the university campus, and discuss my possible acceptance with the school admission staff. My aunt's call gave me an additional boost to study even harder to ensure I could catch up and pass the BAC.

I researched what an actuary was for the rest of that week. My aunt had motivated me by saying that actuaries have a lucrative career, and making a lot of money was extremely important to me. I had no plans for remaining poor and spending my life living in a cité like L'abbaye. I wanted to escape this life of struggle my parents had lived for so long. I wanted a career that offered financial stability.

I discovered that actuaries are business professionals who specialize in quantifying and managing risks in the insurance and financial industries using mathematical and statistical methods. I also learned that I would need to take a series of exams to become a qualified actuary, but I would be paid to take them and receive salary increases for passing them. Everything sounded very doable to me, given that I liked mathematics and wanted to work in the financial sector. The most exciting part was that Aunty Christine was right, actuaries make a lot of money. Fully credentialed Actuaries make between $150,000 to $250,000 annually and can even make more. This fitted the prestigious life I wanted.

The idea of returning to the United States had long been a dream of mine. I had seen the big skyscrapers in downtown Chicago when I was younger, and my dream was to work in one of them one day. I was sold on the idea. My new career goal was now to become an actuary and study in the United States. This decision brought focus to what I was doing and motivation during the long hours at the library. I had a clear goal for what I wanted to do when I graduated, which was my motivation to excel in school and pass the BAC.

I remember the first day when classes resumed. Studying with Adrian and Aria during the summer had helped rebuild my competitive and

_____

"Fully credentialed Actuaries make between $150,000 to $250,000 annually and can even make more. This fitted the prestigious life I wanted."

_____

focused spirit so that I felt unstoppable. I wanted to show my professors that I could come back from the ashes. I sat in front on the first day so as not to let anything or anyone distract me. I knew my time to make up for my shortsightedness was limited, and I could not waste one second. Every student in my class was very competitive. Most students had planned to get into Grandes Écoles, and competition was required. Five students were always on top in class, and Adrian was one of them.

We had close to thirty students in our scientific class. In the previous year, I had probably dropped to one of the five worst-performing students in the class. I was determined to get back to the top. My teachers did not take long to acknowledge my behavior change, and they encouraged me to continue down that path. I often stayed up very late, close to midnight on weekdays, studying and creating flashcards to memorize as much material as possible.

What I found difficult, especially in mathematics, was the topics covered in my senior year were built upon what we had covered in my junior year when I had been less than enthusiastic about school. As a result, I often needed help understanding the foundations, which required extra study effort. With time, the results of months of hard work started paying off.

We had just finished a long week of midterm exams, and the topics covered in the history exam spanned junior and senior year classes. I would often memorize during my 40 minutes train ride to school. I had created hundreds of flashcards for different subjects and was extremely diligent. For that history exam, I had read my flashcards over and over again to make sure I knew the material. I wanted to do exceptionally well because I knew my progress would be highlighted positively on my report card.

Our school had a high ranking based on students' performance in the BAC. The passing rate in the BAC was one of the factors that distinguished schools. We were at a 96-percent passing rate across all sections. The scientific section was at a 98-percent passing rate. Teachers were expected to ensure the students remained motivated to excel at the BAC. Another component of the BAC that counted in the school ratings was how many students would receive honors. To get honors, students must have studied extensively throughout the school year to ensure they can correctly answer most of the questions on the BAC.

Our history teacher wanted our class to do well in that section of the BAC, and every one of our classes was centered around potential questions that could be asked during the BAC. Those midterm graded papers she was about to distribute were almost predetermining where everyone would fall during the BAC—at least for the history section. She habitually distributed graded papers from the top grade to the lowest. Most students, myself included, always hoped that their papers would be returned first. That method of distributing papers was one of her ways of building competition among her students.

To the surprise of all my classmates (and teacher), I received my graded paper third! Only two students had performed better than me. I was so excited, I couldn't wait to get home to tell Mom. I also outperformed in mathematics and reached the top of the class. Fall break was almost here, and I was excited about my Chicago trip. I had regained my confidence in school and was slowly trying to clear my reputation so my teachers would write favorable comments in my senior year report.

DePaul University, a private Catholic university located in Chicago, was the first American university I had ever visited. The main campus of DePaul University is located in the Lincoln Park neighborhood of Chicago.The university also has a second campus in the Loop area of downtown Chicago. My aunt took me to the downtown campus around the skyscrapers I had admired so much while living in Chicago as a child. I recall stepping on the university campus and feeling like I was in one of the American movies. Everything looked so big, and DePaul's downtown campus appeared distinguished and prestigious.

DePaul was also highly ranked in Chicago, so I knew the school had built a prestigious reputation over the years. My senior high school class at St Peter, combining the scientific, literature, and economic sections, was only about 90 students as compared to DePaul's 20,000! I was so impressed by how vast the campus looked. My aunt had already scheduled an appointment with the admissions office so my questions could be answered. I was wholly sold about attending this university; all I wanted to know was what it would take to get in.

The admissions counselor told me I must pass the BAC and earn satisfactory grades in my senior year to gain admission. I gave them by high school report summary to review but no mention of my bad behavior in my prior report cards was made, which I was so glad about. During the rest of my trip to Chicago, I followed my aunt to the library while she was studying. She let me borrow her actuarial science books so that I could become familiar with the subject. I noticed that I was already studying some of the topics covered in her classes on the BAC mathematics segment). This career was well aligned with the skills I wanted to use, and I knew entering this career was the right decision for me. I still had hopes of getting into the French Grandes Écoles, but DePaul University would be my backup plan.

When we returned from the fall break, my teachers wanted to meet with each student individually to discuss their career plans. I had a good plan in place, and I was very excited to hear my teachers' feedback as it would solidify what I already had in mind.

My biology teacher, Madame Beatrice, was not a fan of mine. She was a tall French woman with a constant tan as if she lived in the south of France. She had graduated from a Grande École, and her class was very rigorous. My senior year was my first year of having her as a teacher.

Unfortunately, she had read my last report card, and to her, I meant trouble. I don't think she believed in redemption.

I always felt that Madame Beatrice favored students over me and only focused on students she felt had the greatest chances of matriculating into a Grande École. I did everything to get into her good graces the first trimester to no avail. When my turn came to go to that teachers' meeting, some of the teachers were divided concerning me. Some teachers knew that I was fighting hard to redeem myself while others had no real hope for my future as they felt that my career outcomes would, unfortunately, suffer from the consequences of my past actions. Madame Beatrice was one of them.

During that teachers' meeting, I was asked one question: "what do you want to do as a career?"

I immediately answered with excitement. "I plan to become an actuary. I plan to apply to preparatory classes at Grandes Écoles. If I am not accepted, I will go to the United States for my education."

Madame Beatrice immediately responded, "You do not stand a chance of attending a Grande École. I do not believe that you have enough rigor to become an actuary as well."

Some of the teachers who had known me well over the years believed in me. They did feel I could become an actuary by going the general university route as my chance to Grandes Écoles would be very limited.

The only part of my plan they could all agree on was my going to the United States for my education would be a great beginning for me if I could pass the BAC and be accepted into a university. In fact, some of them did not believe that I could even pass the BAC. Despite the wave of discouragement I felt, I left that meeting with enough exasperation to prove them wrong and succeed. In my heart I knew I had worked hard to demonstrate that I was changing, but at that point, it seemed that the changes I was making was never enough for some of them.

I was determined to prove them wrong. I cried on the train back home. I felt guilty and filled with regret. I told Mom everything that had happened. I was angry at some of my teachers and even at myself, but she said, "You need to understand where they are coming from. You must take responsibility for your past actions while also working hard to take hold of your future career opportunities. Sonya, focus on what you have set your mind to do and prove them wrong! If you focus on the past, you cannot move forward."

I felt like a failure at the bottom of the pack in my class, but my fire did not stop burning.

I created a study plan for the BAC that consisted of spending all my weekends at the library from opening to closing. I also decided to stay back in school on weekdays to study after classes instead of directly returning home. The commute back to Creteil was often tiring, and keeping all the energy I had after my classes was important. Some of our teachers often stayed behind in the teacher's lounge, so I had access to them for any questions. I also loved using the class board to lay out problems and solutions. Aria was not allowed to stay out late, so she couldn't stay after hours with me at the school. However, she committed to joining me every weekend at the library. Adrian always agreed to study with me as he was very competitive. Since Adrian was at the top of our class, I was able to leverage much of his knowledge.

The BAC for the scientific section (BAC S) focused on scientific classes such as mathematics, physics, chemistry, and biology, along with more general classes like philosophy, foreign language, history, and French. Since I chose to have mathematics as a concentration, the mathematics section of the BAC would have a greater weight than some of the other subjects. The weight of each section of the BAC was based on the number of hours allocated to each subject. Math, physics, biology, and chemistry had the highest weight in the science section. I organized my study accordingly to ensure that I would master the subjects with the highest weight first before going down the list. I knew I would perform the worst in the French language, and I needed more time to make up for years of lagging behind in this subject. Since I was good at memorization, I made notecards for all my classes. I carried hundreds of flashcards everywhere and even on bed. I would even fall asleep memorizing them. In the second trimester, my grades started to rebound and became my motivation to know that I was on the right track for the BAC.

My mom came home that trimester with the surprise our family had waited for a very long time. On that memorable Thursday evening, I had just returned from school. Mom had already told my brother her news, but she was eagerly waiting for my sister and me to come home so she could share the good news with us. When we entered the house, she immediately summoned us to the living room. I immediately noticed the radiant smile on her face and that she was holding a key.

"Guess what I want to say!" she said excitedly.

Truly, I had no idea what to think; I just wanted to know what it was. My brother was standing behind her with a big smile. He could not hold back his joy and immediately shouted, "Mom bought a house!"

I froze momentarily because I could not believe my ears. Mom had talked about her plans to buy a home over the years, but with so many bills to pay, I never thought she would be able to achieve that dream. My immediate reaction was that I wanted to see the house, and any house would have been good. I was fed up with L'abbaye and wanted to live far away from public housing. I had associated such a stigma with those buildings over the years that I no longer wanted to be connected to them. I wanted to rise higher and away from what signified shame and struggle for my family.

The timing of when my mom bought our new home could not have been more perfect. I had studied so much that I had reached a point where I needed extra motivation to continue to push until the end. Mom had done it. She had reached one of her lifetime dreams by becoming a homeowner. That same evening, she took us to visit our new home.

Entering our very own home was like a dream come true. We had waited for so long and had talked about it for so long that I didn't believe it would ever become a reality. My mom had planned it and made her dream happen precisely on the five-year mark she had set for herself. She had remained committed to her vision and had worked hard to see it come to pass. I could see the pride on her face. Mom needed to know that she had something of her own and no longer had to depend on the "system." Seemingly, the part of our dignity that had been stripped away by living at L'abbaye had returned to us. I could finally invite my classmates and friends to my home. No more shame was attached to where I lived. Mom's becoming a homeowner motivated me to see my dreams come to pass. I knew because of her that, despite the challenge and difficulties that would come, I would be able to pass the BAC and get into a top actuarial science program.

With the passing of time, my dream to go to the United States started to outweigh my hope of getting into a Grande École. I received my conditional acceptance letter from DePaul University two months before the BAC. I would gain full acceptance once I passed the BAC. One of DePaul University's central selling points was the diversity of its campus—both in terms of students and faculty. DePaul made sure to highlight that fact in its admission packet. I had spent the last six years of my life going to a school that lacked diversity, and I was fed up with never having a teacher who looked like me.

Grandes Écoles were similar to St. Peter in their lack of diversity and ethnic minority backgrounds being underrepresented. Even if I stood a chance of getting into one of these schools, I believe I would have continued to feel that hidden discomfort of "me versus them." Diversity was becoming an important topic to me, and I wanted to be part of a higher institution that believed as I did. It was not just a matter of attending an elite school; I wanted to attend a university that fit with my beliefs. DePaul University was the perfect fit for where I was at that junction in my life.

The primary week when BAC written exams occurred was exhausting, leaving me mentally and physically drained. Each of the exams was between two and four hours long. The science exams were the most stringent and lasted four hours. I knew I did the best in biology, contrary to what Madame Beatrice would have thought. I had almost memorized our entire 300-page biology book. I had studied so much that I believe my brain capacity had expanded exponentially. I could literally read a flashcard and immediately retain the information.

As I had already suspected, the subject I most struggled with was the French language. I blamed it on not growing up reading a lot. I could never fully understand French grammar and how to adequately express myself scholastically in my language. I had built such an insecurity around it that Mom would pay me each time I earned a good grade in French class. She wanted something to motivate me to perfect my French language rather than spend most of my study time on science-related subjects. Nevertheless, it did not seem to matter how much I tried, I knew I had done poorly on both the oral and written section of the French language exam, but because its overall weight was low, I did not worry.

I was quite disappointed in my performance in English foreign language. Given that I had lived and studied in the United States, I was at the top of my class in that subject. However, I found several elements of that exam section challenging. I had hoped for that section to boost my overall score, but I would probably land an average grade.

Over the past months, Adrian had brought up the topic of getting honors on the BAC several times, and the idea had lodged in my mind.

Adrian's love for competition had rubbed off on me. Adrian knew without a doubt that he would receive honors. I wanted to get honors for the mere thought of showing some of my teachers that they were wrong about me, especially Madame Beatrice, who had no faith in my even passing the BAC.

Most students who got into Grandes Écoles received honors on the BAC. So even though I had decided not to apply to one of these schools, earning honors would have been my confirmation that I could have gotten in had I applied. Getting honors on the BAC was my redemption from my rebellious school years and my way of saying, "I may have went astray, but I still ended well."

The BAC results were released a few weeks after the exams were completed. I woke up at four o'clock in the morning unable to sleep. I had spent the past year studying to the best of my ability to redeem my future, knowing that my future indeed depended on it. DePaul University would only admit me if I passed the BAC. I felt as if everyone wanted to see how I would perform. *Will I be able to redeem myself truly?*

For my parents, my BAC results would indicate whether I had truly honored their years of working day and night to ensure that I excelled scholastically. I did not want to fail anyone, but especially them. I wanted to prove that redemption was possible. After all, that was what the police officer expected of me. He told me that if I got back up, it would inspire many rebellious youths to take life seriously and help them see they could also be successful in society.

I was meditating on all these thoughts that morning and almost rehearsing the joy that could be when I found out I had passed the BAC. My gut feeling told me I had passed, but I was still anxious at the idea of maybe having done poorly on certain sections. So much was on the line for me. I got ready by seven o'clock, knowing I had an hour of travel to get to the school where the results would be released. Afterward, the students planned to gather back at St. Peter, where our teachers would meet with us to congratulate us. I wanted to be part of those being congratulated.

I arrived early at the school where the exam results would be released, and only a few students were waiting. I walked around the neighborhood with Aria as we chatted anxiously about our expected results. At that school we would see our names, whether we passed the BAC, and whether we had received honors. I desperately wanted to see honors next to my name as my way of saying thank you to my parents for working so hard for my future.

An hour later, the time had finally come. Aria and I walked back to the school now so packed with students that a line had formed. Someone finally opened the main door, and the students seemed to be almost running to check their results displayed on boards in the school playground. Everything was divided by last name, so I had to find my last name.

I could already hear the joy in students' voices who found they had passed. Before I could get to my name, I heard Adrian excitedly scream, "Yes, I got honors!" I was so scared that I could barely look through the list, but finally I found my name: "Sonya Rolande Mbatchou" and the words: "Passed with Honors." I was so shocked, I almost cried. *This is what redemption feels like!* I could not wait to call my parents, who were expecting to hear from me.

I turned around and saw that Aria was waiting for me. I immediately and tearfully told her, "I have passed with honors. I did it—we did it!" We were so overjoyed because months and months of hard work had paid off. Some of my classmates came to greet me and congratulate me. Many were in shock that I had received honors as only a few in our class did. Most of them had such an excellent track record in high school, receiving honors was almost expected of them.

Despite my past failures, I had still made it to the top. That feeling was inexplicable. I ran outside where there would be less noise to call my mom. She picked up immediately, and I screamed, telling her I had passed with honors.

"Sonya, I knew you would do it. I knew it!" Mom said with much joy.

Mom never had any doubt in her mind that I wouldn't be able to rise higher. I did it! I had met the last requirement for admission at DePaul University. I was rising higher!

Chapter 6

Pursuing My American Dream: Becoming a Fellow Actuary

I landed in Chicago in the summer of 2006. I was 17 years old and had one mission: to become a Fellow of the American Society of Actuaries. Aunt Christine had told me about her close friend, a Fellow Actuary, who had spent years studying for the actuarial exams. She told me he had spent 12 years studying before becoming a Fellow Actuary. Her description of that friend made me feel that he must be a billionaire. My aunt's dream was for me to reach the level that man had attained.

When I arrived in Chicago, my aunt warned me that staying focused and excelling in school were essential for my success. Mom had shared with Aunt Christine about my rebellious years and wanted her to tell me in no uncertain terms would she tolerate such behavior here. "Sonya, your future depends on your being serious and committed to continuing the study habits you followed for the BAC. I am convinced that if you study well, by the time you graduate, you could land a lucrative actuarial job that will pay you while you continue studying to become a Fellow Actuary."

I looked at her and replied with great certainty, "Don't worry. Not only will I get an actuarial job, but I will pass at least two actuarial exams before I graduate."

Actuarial exams are a series of rigorous professional exams every student must take to become a certified actuary. These exams cover topics such as probability theory, mathematical statistics, financial mathematics, and economics that assess the knowledge and skills required to succeed as an Actuary. The actuarial exam series is divided into two primary tracks: the Society of Actuary (SOA) and the Casualty Actuarial Society (CAS). The SOA track focused on life insurance, health insurance, retirement benefits, and financial investment. The CAS track focused on property and casualty insurance.

I wanted to follow the SOA track because I would have the opportunity to do financial mathematics, which is related to the career I had originally planned as a financial engineer. I would need to pass a series of five rigorous exams to reach the first level of certification with the SOA, which would grant me the status of Associate of the Society of Actuary. Then I would need to pass another three lengthy exams to become a Fellow of the Society of Actuary. That journey could take me anywhere from five to ten years after university. Becoming a Fellow Actuary was comparable to pursuing a Ph.D.

Studying for the BAC laid the foundations I needed to excel in this career. That preparation helped develop the competitive spirit I needed to succeed in the actuarial exam system. Actuarial exams are graded on a pass/fail basis, and candidates must be above a certain percentile rank to pass the exam. That percentile rank is determined by an exam committee and varies from exam to exam. Not all candidates will pass; some must fail.

The actuarial exam is incredibly competitive because the pool of candidates is already very educated. Someone must have extensive mathematics abilities to sit for an actuarial exam. So, for me to pass, I would need to do better than many gifted students. I was not intimidated, I was more than prepared for that battle; at least that is what I thought early on in my journey. When my aunt told me the story of her wealthy actuarial friend, I replied, "That will be me one day." She smiled with hope; she wanted my success so badly to be the reality for our family.

I felt like I was seeing what I had watched in American movies my first day at DePaul University. When I entered the school building and saw the lockers in the hallway and the large classrooms, I was slightly intimidated by the size of the school and the abundance of students. I knew I would eventually get used to the size and numbers. Many students had attended my first-year orientation session located on the Lincoln Park campus. We gathered in the large school auditorium, where school officials welcomed us to the campus. As I was about to walk into the auditorium, one beautiful African American student greeted me with a lovely smile. I learned she was a fellow freshman from Detroit, and like me, she was excited to start school. Sanja was very friendly and could see that I seemed overwhelmed by my new environment. Unfortunately, I quickly lost her in the large crowd of students around us. I found a seat somewhere in the back of the room so I could breathe in this new experience without too many people looking at me. I was a little shy.

One of the university staff led in an icebreaker to see which students had traveled the farthest to attend DePaul. He started, "If you are not from Chicago, raise your hand." Of course, I raised my hand. States were mentioned and then foreign countries. You guessed it. I was the one who came from the farthest location, and suddenly all eyes were on me. When I had to stand up to receive a prize, I almost regretted raising my hand.

Even though I spoke English well, I was terrified at the idea of a "real" American hearing my accent and thinking that my English was bad. I was not shy, but coming to the United States on my own to study made me even more introverted. After the icebreaker, one of the university leaders spoke about the university's mission and values.

DePaul University is a Catholic Vincentian university that prepares students to be successful in their chosen fields and agents of transformation throughout their lives. The speaker highlighted how important it was for us to become change agents for our community and society in general. He stressed that DePaul believed that not only are the students called to reach their personal career goals, but also to make a difference in their world.

The school's Vincentian heritage originates from the remarkable lives of Vincent de Paul and Louise de Marillac, who were French like me. They lived a life of service, worked for the common good, and built a just and equitable society. The fire to become a change agent was ignited in me on that day. I knew I was in the right place at the right time. I realized there was a bigger purpose for my being in this school.

I was amazed at how DePaul pushed the importance of service even more than studying. One of the major burdens in my heart was to become a change agent for youth in places like my former neighborhoods: Air-Bel, Chicago's South Side, and L'abbaye. That vision had been ignited after my encounter with that police officer. I wanted to inspire other minorities in my field and beyond. I told myself that day that I would succeed in my career and go back to those places to inspire the youth to rise higher.

I majored in mathematical science with a concentration in actuarial science. In the first year of my actuarial program, I was required to take calculus and multi-calculus courses as a prerequisite for actuarial classes the following year. The actuarial classes would cover topics that were tested on actuarial exams. Many science students, such as biology or physics majors, also had calculus as a pre-requisite for their major classes, so my calculus classes freshmen year were always large and full. I quickly noticed in my first couple of classes that very few Black students were in these classes. I was accustomed to seeing few Black students in science given the limited number of Black students at St. Peter, but I was not expecting to see the same disparity in such a large school like DePaul.

Despite the diversity in DePaul's student body, I felt that my math courses needed more diversity. From the first few weeks I was at DePaul,

I told myself that I would not become bothered by what seemed to be some lack of diversity in STEM because I knew I would eventually do something about that need. It did not intimidate me, but it was something I was determined to change. Instead of dwelling on the shortage, I stayed focused on excelling in all of my classes. I had already covered calculus in my high school, so I was always at the top of the class. Because of my focus and competitive spirit, I also excelled in all of my other classes, and doing well boosted my confidence as a student.

I used the same study strategy from high school of developing a study plan and then executing that plan at the school library. My calculus teacher, who taught the calculus 1 to 3 series, was a fan of mine. I was the student who always sat in the front of the class and participated whenever she asked questions. Having teachers who believed in me like the ones at DePaul was a breath of fresh air to me. I had left St. Peter feeling a little discouraged with guilt and without the blessing of some of my teachers. At DePaul, my professors really believed in me, but in all fairness to my St. Peter teachers, DePaul only knew the "new me." They truly believed that I could become what I had set to achieve in my future. DePaul was my fresh start; I knew I had a clean start here. By the end of the first trimester, I was singled out by the mathematics department for my superior performance in my math courses, and many professors encouraged me to become a math tutor.

The math department was located on the fifth floor of the science building. Math tutors worked in a small room in the far back of that department. Chalkboards were on multiple walls of the department that students and professors could use to solve math problems. I loved tutoring math. I had always been told that the best way to master a subject was to teach it. I tutored calculus during my first year, and multiple students came to my tutoring hours. My "class" became so full that we had to move to the hallway. Many of the mathematic professors started to notice the

Black student with an accent teaching other students calculus. Within months, most of the instructors in the department knew my name without my ever introducing myself. "Being different" made me stand out, and I believe those in the math department wanted to see someone like me thrive in their field. I also felt very included despite being one of the few minorities.

One day, an African American student came to learn more about who I was. She told me that she had never seen a Black student like me with superior abilities in mathematics, and I was inspiring her to push through and declare herself as a math major.

Wanting to know more about her, I asked, "Are you from Chicago?"

"I grew up on the west side of Chicago in the Austin neighborhood. I have never seen a Black woman pursue a career in mathematics, but I have always had a passion for math. I'm an undeclared major, and I've been taking various courses to determine the best path for me."

I immediately encouraged her to look into careers with a mathematics degree, including becoming an actuary. Unknown to me, she shared with her mathematics professor, Dr. Karina, who taught her algebra, what I had encouraged her to do. That professor then reached out to me for an opportunity to mentor more students.

Dr. Karina, a very tall Russian lady, encouraged me to join the math club and even run for office so I could inspire other students to follow mathematics-related careers. Dr. Karina focused on teaching pure mathematics and wanted to see more women earn a doctoral degree in mathematics. She and I connected right away as we were both fascinated by our love for mathematics and desired to see more diversity in our field.

As I met with Dr. Karina that same week, she shared some of her goals for the Math Club. As the academic chairperson for the group, she planned to encourage math students to attend more conferences and invite outside speakers working in related fields. Encouraged by her vision, I immediately ran for office as secretary. At the most, 20 students were involved in the Math Club, with only half of them fully involved. Seven of us attended Dr. Karina's presentation to the Math Club on discrete mathematics and its applications. Despite the low attendance, I felt the group was quite interactive. I introduced myself to the club president and mentioned my desire to run for office in the group. He said no one was contending for that office, so I most likely would get the position. I was more than excited and started planning ideas for the following academic year and gathering resources to execute Dr. Karina's vision for the club.

Even though my official involvement in the Math Club board would only start in my sophomore year, I wanted to find ways to expand the club and get more students in joining our events. After receiving approval, I started contacting corporations with math-related professionals, such as Statisticians and Actuaries. I combed through their website, looking for contacts and emails. I asked Dr. Karina to read through my introductory emails to ensure I represented the DePaul Math department well.

Allen, an actuary working for one of the major insurance companies in Chicago, reached out to me almost immediately. The company was looking to hire actuarial students, and he hoped to determine whether DePaul students would be a good fit for what the company needed. He also thought meeting with the Math Club would be a great way to introduce his organization and promote the actuarial profession. The Math Club president then asked me to organize the meet and greet for the club. Allen and I coordinated everything, including an event date before the school year ended. He would come with an HR representative to spend two hours on our campus. The goal would be to present themselves and the opportunities their company offered and meet with students interested in working there. I printed flyers and contacted everyone on the Math Club email list. I felt as if I was already performing my role as secretary. I was also able to obtain pizzas for the event since I knew food was a major enticement to attract students to attend.

I still remember the day Allen and I first met each other. He had my phone contact information should he find navigating DePaul's campus challenging. I knew finding the math department could be difficult. Allen did get lost, and he did call me for directions. I had set up the meeting in one of the math department rooms, and with some students already waiting, the event already looked very promising.

When Allen and his HR rep arrived on the fifth floor, I heard the math department secretary greet them from afar, so I knew they had found their way. Allen was an African American actuary who had decided to get involved in recruiting to diversify the talent pool at his organization. I did not know he was Black before meeting him, so meeting became even more exciting for me. I waved at them from afar and told them to come to the back, where the meeting room was.

The biggest smile spread across his face as if he had won the jackpot! I believe he was excited to see that I was Black as well, and we immediately connected. He greeted me with a hug, and I showed the two men where to hang their jackets. I helped them set up their laptop on the projector when we got to the room. By the time they were about to start, close to 20 students were already present. We even had to bring in extra chairs. The event was already looking like a success—whether the attendees came for the food or the talk.

Allen explained that most insurance companies were looking for students who had passed at least one or two actuarial exams by graduation as a way of filtering out those who could not endure the rigor of future exams. He also shared the importance of doing an internship while still in school to significantly increase our chances of getting a job. He encouraged us to take courses other than mathematics or actuarial science such as accounting, finance, and computer science to diversify our skillset and be more versatile. Many students came with their résumés, but I did not. I was only a freshman and did not think I would qualify for anything; I simply wanted to learn what companies were looking for in actuarial students.

Allen had extra time after the meeting, and he asked me if I was free, so we could discuss more about becoming an actuary. I definitely was interested. His HR rep had to leave when the event concluded, so I met with Allen only. I could tell Allen was hoping to get me into his company. He wanted to see more of us in the actuarial profession, and during our conversation, he shared about the International Association of Black Actuaries (IABA).

I had never heard of this organization, and he added that he was a member and a coordinator for their Chicago affiliate activities. He explained that the IABA existed to support and celebrate Black actuarial students and actuaries. He believed that connecting with the IABA could help me advance as an actuarial student. I shared with him how excited I was to hear of this organization, given that I had never met a Black actuarial student or actuary. I responded, "I have noticed a need for more diversity in STEM fields, and one of my dreams is to help effect change in the future."

"Sonya, the IABA would be the perfect organization for you to get involved with since the organization shares a similar vision. Also, take an actuarial exam as soon as possible."

I had initially planned to wait until my junior year to take actuarial exams, but Allen explained that I could take any of the first two exams, Probability or Financial Mathematics, right away. "All you need to do is get related study materials. Some schools with larger actuarial programs have students taking exams in their first or second year."

Immediately my competitive spirit kicked in, and I said, "I will be taking one in my sophomore year."

"I can't tell you how important it is for actuarial students to realize early on how intense the exams will be. I've only passed two exams so far, and I'm studying while working—a typical schedule for most actuaries."

As we concluded our meeting, we agreed that I would let him know how my first actuarial exam went, and he would add me to the Chicago IABA mailing list. Talking to Allen had been a breath of fresh air. I was excited to meet an actuary in person, and not only that, he also looked like me! Our meeting made my becoming an actuary even more realistic.

When I had applied to DePaul, neither Mom nor I realized how expensive American schools were. We somehow thought I could get scholarships, which was one of the reasons why I had worked so hard to maintain a perfect GPA my first year. However, we eventually faced a bill of nearly $20,000 for my first year. I found a part-time job tutoring math to middle school students while also working in the math department. However, I only earned enough to pay a small portion of the tuition with school fees, books, transportation, and some living expenses. Aside from getting student loans, I knew I would need a long-term solution.

I decided to pitch myself to the Office of the Dean based on what I knew the school valued. I scheduled an appointment with the Associate Dean of the Science Department, and I prepared reasons why DePaul should invest in me. I did not know that the Associate Dean was an African American woman, though I did not believe our being Black mattered because I knew the leadership at DePaul wanted to advance the school's diversity and continue promoting community engagement.

At our meeting, I explained to the Associate Dean that I was one of the few Black students in the math department and had maintained a perfect 4.0 GPA throughout my first year. "I have noticed the lack of diversity in science-related courses and the need for DePaul to promote science careers and education throughout its campus and more predominantly Black communities. I would like to volunteer to become a student advocate for the school to help bridge that diversity gap. I promise to maintain a high GPA and remain committed to further diversity in STEM careers."

She was impressed by my pitch and did not ask for more information. I also told her that my sister would be starting at DePaul the following academic year as a biology and mathematics major and that she would commit to the same goal of supporting DePaul in diversifying its STEM student body. "Sonya, I will see what I can do and contact you within a month."

In less than one week I heard back from the Office of the Dean in an email stating they had created and issued a full-tuition scholarship for both my sister and me to cover our full university degree. The leadership was impressed with my passion for advancing diversity within the department, and they encouraged me to continue following the Vincentian values of the university. Just like that, my family and I would not have to worry about how we would afford our college education. I felt empowered to make a difference by seeing DePaul invest so much in my sister and me. The university did not simply preach a message of being the change we wanted to see in our world; the leadership truly lived their founders' principles. They believed that we would one day make a difference for minorities within our respective fields.

During the first trimester of my sophomore year, I started looking for organizations where my sister and I could begin our goal of encouraging Black youth to pursue STEM careers, and we found St. Miguel's Mentoring, Inspiring, and Leading Education (SMILE). DePaul was heavily involved in SMILE, a program utilizing students to tutor and mentor middle school youth in the Austin Chicago neighborhood.

I was unfamiliar with the Austin neighborhood of Chicago, but I had heard about it from the student I mentored in the math department.

I discovered Austin, which had a predominantly Black or African American population, was located on the west side of Chicago. Close to one-third of the individuals in that neighborhood lived below the poverty level, and the community was also marked by high crime rates. Those statistics looked quite similar to the demographics of Chicago's South Side.

St. Miguel School's Gary Comer campus was in Austin, and the goal of that school was to enroll underserved students from low-income families who had already fallen behind. DePaul students tutored there every Saturday morning. The timing worked well with my sister's and my schedule, and my college friend Sanja, who also decided to volunteer there as she had a passion for serving underserved students. The SMILE program was vital, especially for children who lived in environments exposed to delinquency. I planned to tutor students in mathematics and stir their interest in STEM careers such as actuarial science. I also thought their relating with Black students who could mentor them and inspire them would be of the utmost importance.

I looked forward to SMILE every week. While there, we would tutor the students for a few hours, talk to them, and sometimes play basketball. Brad, the program director, was very passionate about the youth who attended. He constantly encouraged the three of us to come every week. "These students are so blessed to see collegiate Black women spending time with them. I can see the difference you are making in the lives of these students. Some of these students, who used to attend infrequently, began to attend SMILE more consistently."

Deborah, a young African American, was one who began to attend regularly. She loved math and always excelled at solving the math problems we worked on together. I would often pitch careers in mathematics to her and encourage her to be focused in school so that she could earn a scholarship to a good college or university. She was interested in DePaul since she would see us come every week. Deborah's grades in math rose from Cs to mainly As and Bs after only a couple of months of being tutored. Brad kept sharing good reports about the student performance from their involvement in SMILE.

I could tell that the students who attended became very attached to us. They graduated from simply waving when we arrived to embracing us. The smiles on their faces every time our bus would drop us off meant everything. Some arrived early enough to ensure they could spend every second of their time there with us. Our eyes were opened to how much of an impact we could have—especially with that age group.

The bus ride back to DePaul from SMILE was sometimes quiet as we meditated on our impact on the students and the changes we were seeing by simply sacrificing a Saturday morning. Being involved in SMILE had a significant impact on all of us, and our volunteering there is how I became a close friend to Sanja. I discovered we shared many common visions for the future. Sanja was a real-estate major who had come to study in Chicago from Detroit. She dreamed of developing many Chicago and Detroit underserved communities through commercial real estate. As an African American, she was passionate about causes that would positively impact predominantly Black neighborhoods like Austin. Amazingly, we had this vision in common even though we came from different countries.

Even though I had been reared in another country, I found many commonalities in terms of the challenges predominantly African American communities faced in the United States and what predominantly African-immigrant communities faced in France. I wanted to be a change agent for good and invest back into these communities.

In the same way I was mentoring the students at SMILE, I also had my mentor. Allen was encouraging me to take an actuarial exam in my sophomore year. I had completed all the prerequisites I needed after taking summer courses, so I had begun taking actuarial classes during my sophomore year. One actuarial class, Financial Mathematics (FM), had been structured to cover the material in the FM actuarial exam, a multiple-choice exam covering the time value of money, interest rate models, bond valuation, and derivative instruments. With much study, I was doing well in the class. Interestingly, this class, which covered topics that I truly loved—finance and mathematics—was the primary reason why I chose actuarial science as a career.

Professor Gianus from Greece taught our actuarial science classes with much passion. He never became a certified actuary but always encouraged every student to take the exams. Something about actuarial exams both excited and terrified us at the same time. Since our professor had never taken any of them, we always felt they must be hard to pass.

Professor Gianus liked me as a student because of my class participation and my being prepared. I would read whatever the class covered beforehand to stay focused. I wanted to ask all the questions I would need to pass the FM exam, which I planned to take with other classmates at the end of that trimester. My goal was to score a 6 out of 10, the minimum to pass.

I was doing well in class and receiving As in all the class assignments. One of my classmates taking the FM with us purchased a study manual that he shared with us. We all studied with it. The study manual was intimidating and covered much more than what we had in class. I was more focused on following the class material than the study manual. Still, I aimed to do the practice exam question the Society of Actuary had posted on their website. *If I can get just As in the class and do well on the practice questions, then I should be able to score at least a 6 on that exam to pass.*

The FM exam was scheduled toward the end of our first trimester. I was studying with two of my actuarial class members, Adam and Janet, for the exam. They enjoyed my company as I always motivated them to study more. I lived a couple of blocks from the school, and they both knew I would be at the library late in the evenings and on weekends. Adam and Janet knew if they hung out with me, they would be focused enough to study for the exam.

Actuarial students were recommended to study at least 100 hours for each hour of exam. The FM exam was a 3-hour exam, so the recommendation was to study at least 300 hours for that exam. Technically, we included the hours we were already studying for our actuarial class as part of the exam study hours; however, we were still far behind the 300-hours threshold. We were not discouraged, knowing the two weeks before the exam would be the most intense.

During those two weeks, I realized exactly how hard the exam would be. When I started doing the practice questions the Society of Actuaries posted on their website, I realized these questions were different from the exam questions Professor Gianus gave us to solve on exams. I thought they were ten times harder. I needed an entire day to solve only three practice questions! I knew I was in trouble as I had to answer 35 questions in only 3 hours during the FM exam.

My only hope was that during the actual FM exam, I would be asked only questions I had already covered while studying. Janet and Adam were even more behind than I was. They were struggling in our class, but they still wanted to take the FM exam to ensure they had a taste of what it would take to become certified Actuaries.

On the actual exam day, we all met at the lobby of one major insurance company, where the exam will take place. Allen worked at that company, so he told me he would meet me after I had finished my exam to check on me. Allen had passed the FM exam the previous year, and he had given me tips on how to study for that exam based on his own experience. Despite my challenges of studying for the FM exam, I still came on exam day very hopeful.

We saw a series of signs posted for "Actuarial Exam FM" in the lobby, so we followed the arrows to a large conference room that had been organized with study tables and chairs. Two people would sit at one table, and the tables were evenly spaced. In the front was a long table where the proctors sat. At least 100 people planned to take the exam that day. We had to wait in line to show our I.D., our exam confirmation number, and hand them our calculator to reset.

The entire process was terrifying. I could feel the fear of failing permeating the room. I noticed many had note cards they were scanning for the final time. Most of us looked stressed. We all understood the reality of how actuarial exams were structured. Some of us will pass; some of us will fail. The answer to the question, "Did we study better than the average student?" would soon be answered.

My competitive spirit was hopeful that I would be one of the top passing students, and I had done my due diligence to memorize and study as much as I could for the exam. After checking in, I chose a table and sat down. I could not stop trembling in fear. As I glanced around me, everyone in the room seemed so serious. I could tell the actuarial exams were no joke.

One of the exam proctors stood and asked us to put aside our belongings. Only our pencils, calculator, and a water bottle were allowed on the table. The room became deathly quiet, and I looked around to see how many of us there were. Every seat was filled, and I also noticed I was the only Black person in the room and that boosted me even more to do well on the exam.

At three hours on the dot, the proctor stood up and told us to put down our pencils and place the exam papers in the provided envelope. It would take about two months for the exams to be graded, and we could check our scores online then. I knew I had given my all during that exam, but somehow, I knew I had failed.

Taking the FM exam truly humbled me, showing me how diligent I would need to be to become an Actuary. I thought I was smart but realized I was simply a local champion who needed to strategize better by completing more practice questions, as well as mastering specific topics about which I was still unsure. Since I had a feeling that I had most likely failed the exam, I spent the following months studying for that exam again.

Janet, Adam, and I had memorized most of the questions asked in our FM exam seating, so we reviewed them with Professor Gianus, who gave us some hints on how we could have solved them. He also encouraged us to review past exams posted on the Society of Actuaries website so that we would be more prepared next time. Janet and Adam told me they would retake the exam if they failed after graduating. That exam was only offered twice yearly, during the spring and fall. Janet and Adam were both seniors and had waited until their senior year to take actuarial classes. I was the youngest in my class, but Allen had advised me to take as many actuarial exams as possible in college. During the fall break, I continued studying independently for the FM exam. I knew I had failed it despite not seeing the results, and I did not want to waste time.

The exam results were released on a Friday in the following January. I had indeed failed the exam with a terrible score—scoring 2 out of a possible 10—even worse than I had imagined. Even Janet and Adam, who had not studied as much for it, performed better than I did—even though they also failed.

I called Mom for encouragement and told her what I thought was bad news. I cried uncontrollably, telling her I did not have what it took to become an Actuary. I cried because I had done so poorly despite how much I had studied. I felt as if my dream of becoming an actuary would be unachievable. "Mom, I need to be more intelligent to pass those exams! I hoped I would score a 4 or a 5 out of 10, but only getting 2 crushed me. Performing worse than Janet and Adam is also difficult for me to swallow. I am at the top of our actuarial class; why did I fail the actuarial exam so miserably?"

Mom comforted me as best she could. "Sonya, we can achieve nothing great without working hard for it. I will always say that you will be the greatest Actuary on earth. Never forget how smart you are! You are a genius! Remember how hard you worked to pass the BAC? You need to find the same motivation you had to pick yourself up from this failure."

I knew I needed to try at least once more. Mom's words of encouragement made me stop crying and start planning. Immediately after hanging up, I emailed Allen to tell him I had failed and asked him for some study tips to be better prepared.

He responded, "I failed the first time I took the test too. After wisely structuring my time, I passed the second time. Don't get discouraged." He shared some tips with me and encouraged me to start studying again. The next couple of months were busy with studying for my classes while studying to retake the FM exam that spring. *This time will be different.*

I developed a strategy of studying the exam material while simultaneously solving many practice problems. I felt as if I were taking the BAC once again. I spent day and night studying, feeling I could not afford to fail. I believed what I was doing was bigger than myself. Mom and Dad had sacrificed too much for me to give up now. My professors, classmates, mentors, and DePaul believed in me and had invested so much in me. I could not—would not—fail them. I could not fail myself.

Every walk I took to the library felt like a destiny walk. I knew this journey to become an Actuary was bigger than me. By studying and eventually passing these actuarial exams, I was fulfilling something bigger. DePaul's library became special to me—a place where I was fulfilling my dream. While studying there, I would dream of what I would become and what my family would achieve. I would dream of the joy in my parents' hearts from seeing their children succeed.

Each time I entered that library to study, I dreamed bigger and bigger aspirations. That fire I had nurtured within was the fire I needed to pass those actuarial exams. When the time came to retake the FM exam, I was ready, and I knew it. I was the only one in my actuarial class taking the exam, and I felt as if I was taking it for all of us. If I passed, I believed they would also be encouraged to pass it. I knew many were cheering me on.

I entered that exam room fired up, tackling each question as if it was a war that I was fighting. I had no doubt that I would pass that exam. Each part of my being was battling to make it to the top. This time, I did not even consider whether anyone looked like me. I knew staying focused would make the difference. I knew with each exam, I was shifting the statistics and making a difference. All I needed was to focus, and I did. I knew when I left the exam room that I had passed. The results only came out two months later, but I knew that something had shifted within my being, and I knew without a doubt that I was called to become an Actuary.

Passing the FM exam gave me such a boost. Everyone celebrated me as if I had passed for them all, but I knew I still had a long way to go—a total of eight exams to become a Fellow Actuary.

Allen encouraged me to attend the IABA annual conference that summer to celebrate Black actuaries and honor the new Black Associates and Fellow Actuaries. Up to that point, my busyness with my classes and exams had prevented my involvement in any of the events the IABA held in Chicago that year.

That summer I had planned to visit my dad in D.C., where he now lived, and the IABA meeting would be held in D.C. as well. I knew

———————

"I knew with each exam, I was shifting the statistics and making a difference. All I needed was to focus, and I did."

———————

Allen was a part of the group, so I told him that I would register to attend. Before attending that conference, I had read very little about the organization. I planned to network as much as possible to seek an internship for the following year. With one actuarial exam passed, I had something in the game to draw attention to recruiters. I prepared my résumé and had a career counselor at DePaul review it. I was prepared to face the world of Actuaries.

I still remember walking into the Westin Hotel and seeing the lobby filled with Black professionals there for the IABA meeting. I saw smiles and joy written on the faces of all the delegates. An IABA representative welcomed me and led me to the place to register. I wore a suit that day and carried a professional bag that held my cell phone, notebook and résumés. At registration, a representative collected my information and gave me the program book to familiarize myself with the events of the next two days.

A student information session was scheduled that morning, followed by a series of talks on different topics impacting the industries in which actuaries work. I met Allen at the student session, and he introduced me to some actuaries attending. I quickly noticed that actuaries had their titles on their badges. Their name was followed by ASA, ACAS, FSA, or FCAS. If the designation started with an "A," they were Associates, the designation given by the Society of Actuary (ASA) or Casualty Actuarial Society (ACAS) for passing the preliminary actuarial exams.

Those with the designation starting with "F" were Fellow Actuaries, who had completed all the actuarial exams within the SOA (FSA) or CAS (FCAS). Every time I saw someone with one of those titles, I would stare long at them in amazement. I was so excited to meet people who were where I was dreaming of going. Their being Black also made a huge difference to me. I had never been in a room with so many successful Black professionals, let alone so many involved in STEM.

Growing up, I did not even know this world could exist. Being at the IABA conference made becoming an actuary so palatable and so possible for me. I could identify myself in those I was seeing and meeting. *If they did it, then I can do it too.* The conference had many exciting presentations, and I got to network with very successful actuaries during the multiple networking sessions. They readily gave me much advice, which aligned with what Allen had shared with me. The highlight of that conference for me was IABA Awards banquet celebrating new Black Associates and Fellow Actuaries.

I arrived at the IABA Awards banquet wearing the same professional black suit I had worn throughout the day. I did not know that IABA Awards banquet was like a red-carpet affair, celebrating true stars. Everyone looked so chic and beyond amazing that night. Most of the attendees had changed and were wearing their best attire. I knew that night would be special, and indeed, it was. After we had finished eating, the celebratory ceremony began.

Somehow the atmosphere shifted in the room. All eyes turned toward the speaker, who explained the purpose of the awards and the impact the IABA was trying to make on the actuarial profession. Then one by one, the names of the new SOA and CAS Associates were called. Everyone cheered with joy each time a name was called.

I was most impacted when the five people who had become Fellow Actuaries were honored. Two of them were beautiful Black women who looked like celebrities to me. When their names were called, they all received a standing ovation. The President of the IABA was in front to welcome them and to pose for a picture with them holding their IABA awards. People clapped, cheered, and screamed for joy as each Fellow Actuary was being called.

I was so amazed. I saw myself in each of these women and reaching that goal seemed more doable for me. Celebrating these Black Actuaries was something I had never before seen. They had reached a level I had never seen people around me attain while growing up. Seeing these Black Actuaries made me believe I could be that person. This conference became the motivation and inspiration I needed to endure the rigor of actuarial exams. I was not in this race to lose; I somehow saw my finish line through their successes. The IABA made the reality of one day becoming a Black Fellow Actuary possible, and I am forever thankful to this organization for that vision.

Chapter 7

I Almost Fell Back; I Almost Gave Up

I had bagged an additional actuarial exam and was almost guaranteed to be offered an actuarial internship. I was living the dream my parents had fought so hard to attain. At DePaul, I soon became a celebrity in the math department. Everyone knew me and loved me. I organized corporate networking events for actuarial students and promoted careers in mathematics to minority students at DePaul and beyond. I had also become a mentor to the underrepresented in sciences. I was doing exactly what I had promised the Associate Dean I would do. My personal dream was my passion, and I was on a mission. I returned from the IABA meeting with a drive to succeed and to make a difference in my field. The Math Club grew from having few participants to filling the room at every event.

Dr. Karina encouraged me to attend the Infinite Possibilities Conference (IPC) held at UCLA. The IPC was created to support minority women interested in mathematics and statistics. Dr. Karina also wanted me to pursue a Ph.D. in mathematics, and the IPC conference had been created by minority women to promote Ph.D. pursuit in either mathematics or statistics.

Even though I had no plans to pursue a doctorate since I was focused on becoming a Fellow Actuary, I decided to attend to encourage other minority students I was mentoring to pursue higher degrees in mathematics or statistics. My sister, two of my mentees, and I decided to attend the IPC conference, and the Math Department provided the funding for our travel.We had all developed a closeness over the past year as they had become more involved in the Math Club. Knowing we were minorities studying mathematics cemented our special bond. We were a source of motivation for one another.

While preparing for this conference, the IPC conference committee informed me that I was a nominee for an IPC college scholarship. This scholarship is given to students committed to mentoring and increasing diversity in the mathematical sciences. The committee informed me that I would be interviewed in person before the winner was selected. This nomination spurred my curiosity to look more into the lives of those women with Ph.D. degrees who had founded and were leading the IPC.

I realized they were all committed to passing the torch and multiplying themselves in others. I saw a zeal in each of them to increase minorities' access to and participation in the mathematical sciences. They most likely had seen, as I had over the years, the lack of diversity in our fields. They were doing exactly what I was trying to achieve, and their lives and mission through the IPC well represented the type of impact I wanted to make in my future. I wanted to become an excellent actuary, but I realized that fulfilling my dream would have no meaning if I did not use my platform to replicate myself.

That realization was already compelling me to do as much as possible at DePaul through the Math Club and SMILE to encourage and support minority students. When the scholarship committee eventually interviewed me, I told them I had researched each of them and could see myself in them. "What you are doing is what I want to do eventually." They had reached their peak of their career and had become role models for many other minority women. I wanted to do the same, and I believed I had the ambition and drive. "No matter how long the journey will be to become a Fellow Actuary, I will make it. I will ensure that I mentor and

"I wanted to become an excellent actuary, but I realized that fulfilling my dream would have no meaning if I did not use my platform to replicate myself."

inspire other minorities to follow a similar path."

I could tell my speech had dazzled them, and within me, I knew I was setting up accountability for myself so I would not give up on my promise. I had made a promise to my mother that I would not return to France empty-handed, I had told the Associate Dean at DePaul that the scholarship they awarded me would not be in vain, and I had now made myself accountable to these distinguished women of the IPC. One day I would join their ranks and work like they were to mentor other minorities.

I was awarded the IPC college scholarship at the conference held at UCLA. When they presented the award, they stated some of the goals I had shared to increase access to careers in mathematics for minorities. The room was filled with existing and future women with an earned Ph.D. in mathematics or statistics. They would all hold me accountable for whether I fulfilled my goals. I had set the bar so high for myself, and I had no doubt that I could reach my goals.

Actuarial internships were essential for those who want to pursue an actuarial career. Internships provide an opportunity to gain hands-on experience in the actuarial field and learn about what an actuary does daily. These internships are also a great way to network with industry professionals and form relationships that could support growth as actuaries. To top it off, internships are usually the straight route to securing a full-time job, and actuarial students with internships on their résumés are usually paid more when they start working full-time.

As now Math Club President, I invited actuaries to talk about their actuarial internship program, which usually operated throughout the summer. This was also an opportunity to get an internship and introduce myself to a potential recruiter. Most actuaries work for insurance companies. Allen's company was not looking for additional interns for the upcoming summer, but some great insurance companies were still hiring in the area. One such company was LallyInsurance. one of the biggest insurance companies at the time and indeed prestigious to work for them. Their actuarial program was known to be very competitive as they usually hired actuarial students from schools with very large programs. These students usually have at least three to four actuarial exams passed by graduation.

Zach, an Actuary with LallyInsurance, and I immediately connected. He was an alumni of DePaul and excited to see so many actuarial enthusiasts in the Math Club. Zach encouraged me to apply for their internship program and gave me an overview of LallyInsurance's very competitive internship program. Since the company was located in one of Chicago's suburbs, the interns were housed in a nearby fashionable hotel and received a generous pay. Many activities and outings were organized for the interns to ensure they had an enjoyable time while working at LallyInsurance. The idea was to make the internship so attractive as compared to their competitors that these interns would want to return to work for them full-time. I could barely contain my excitement!

Zach passed me to the next round of interviews after meeting me in the Math Club. He felt I had the mathematical and leadership skills needed to do well in his company. I met with Allen and DePaul's career counselors to prepare for my in-person interview with LallyInsurance. I memorized every detail I found online about LallyInsurance and its actuarial program to assure my interview proceeded smoothly.

LallyInsurance arranged transportation for the day of my interview. As I waited in the lobby for my ride to arrive, I received a call to come outside. When I walked outside the entrance door, I discovered that LallyInsurance had arranged for a limousine to pick me up. I was so excited that I ran back upstairs and woke my sister to come to see it. *I am living more than the American dream!* My siblings and I had always associated limousines with wealth, and we could not believe that I would be riding in one!

The ride to LallyInsurance was long, but I felt like I was living in a fairytale. I had no doubt in my mind that I would not want to work at the company. LallyInsurance signified prestige to me. I was determined to do everything well during my interview.

I met with several actuaries that day and had a lunch interview with an Actuarial Director. They all gave me an overview of the different departments where actuaries worked and explained how their rotational program worked. Every two years, the actuaries rotated between different departments until they completed the actuarial exam process. They could then settle into one of their preferred departments.

LallyInsurance had a team that worked on Asset Liability Management (ALM), which was my preferred area of interest. The ALM team managed the company's assets and liabilities to maximize its profitability while minimizing its exposure to market risks, such as interest rate and credit risk. ALM was precisely the type of career I wanted to have as an actuary that intersected with the financial market. What excited me even more about their ALM team was that a Black Actuary named Thierry was working there.

I learned that Thierry also came from France and was an African immigrant. Knowing we had very similar cultural backgrounds was a pleasant coincidence. He was the only Black actuary working at Lally, and I was excited about the potential to work with another Black actuary as there were very few in the industry. Thierry would be like having a big brother, which greatly mattered to me.

I chatted briefly with Thierry, and he shared great points about his team and the company. Overall, I did very well interviewing and networking with the different actuaries in that company. Upon returning home that day, I received an email from Zach that the team was impressed and that I would hear back from them soon. Not only was LallyInsurance the dream job for me but for my family as well. I was sold as the job epitomized what succeeding in America looked like to my family. I heard back that same week that I was selected to be an actuarial intern.

My actuarial internship with LallyInsurance was part of my parents' dream for us. They always wanted us to have opportunities they never had and for big doors to open for us. The hotel where the interns stayed was amazing. We enjoyed a buffet breakfast every day and some free dinners at times. My large studio featured a full kitchen, a big bed, and a large-screen television. I felt like a celebrity living in this fully paid for beautiful room for the summer, and I was the envy of my classmates and family.

My mother traveled to Chicago that summer to see us, and I planned for her to stay with me at the hotel. I wanted Mom to see in a tangible way that her labor had not been in vain, that I had changed for the better, and I was doing what she could be proud of. I picked up Mom at the train station near the hotel as I was unable to go to the city to meet her. My sister had dropped her at Union Station in Chicago, ensuring she took the right train. On our walk to the hotel, Mom and I reminisced how thankful we were to have come that far from our years of struggling. We laughed together, thinking about our housing condition in that one-bedroom apartment at L'abbaye. That season of our lives was difficult, but looking back, we found many reasons to laugh about that time.

As we entered the hotel, I could see that Mom was both dazzled and amazed by how nice the accommodations were. I could see the joy in her eyes and the fulfillment in her heart. When we entered my hotel room, she sat quietly on the edge of my bed and kept repeating one word: "Wonderful." I realized she was breathing in what was happening to me. I could see she was so proud of me and that what I was living was precisely what she had dreamed—if not more.

The type of accommodation LallyInsurance had provided was no big deal to the average intern, but to my family, living here was a luxury we had never enjoyed. People living in L'abbaye or Air-Bel were rarely exposed to these opportunities. Knowing that my family was once homeless and had lived in deplorable public housing...and I was now being provided a luxurious hotel room for free was more than a dream for me. This victory meant so much to my family and me. All we talked about during her stay was LallyInsurance.

That night she talked openly to me. "Sonya, continue to follow the path you are on and stay focused. You will be an inspiration to so many young people in France, especially in places where we come from. Never return to your old ways."

"Mom, you can trust me to remain focused and persevere in my career," I insisted.

Mom encouraged me to stay focused, work hard in school, and make a difference in my world. "Don't take what you have been given for granted. Don't forget where we came from and how far we have come."

I kept the promise I made to my mom that summer. I was diligent during my internship and networked with almost all the actuaries at LallyInsurance. I wanted to learn and be inspired by their stories. I bonded closer to Thierry, who became like my "big brother." He connected me with almost everyone from his team and guided me to complete my internship projects and presentation successfully.

Seeing how ambitious Thierry was motivated me. He was not only a Fellow Actuary but had earned many other financial certifications. His being at LallyInsurance was one of the major reasons I wanted to work there full-time. I would have the backing of a big brother. Not only was he Black like me, but we shared the same career interest and came from the same cultural background. We related in so many aspects.

When the internship ended, we were told that only a few would be selected for full-time roles. The 2008 financial crisis had significantly impacted the job market, including the number of full-time offers extended to interns. Many companies were forced to downsize or freeze hiring due to financial pressures and uncertainties.

Nevertheless, I was contacted and extended a full-time offer a month after completing my internship. I did not hesitate to accept the offer. The internship experience had been so positive I did not entertain a single doubt in my mind that I would not want to work there. I knew Thierry and some of the other actuaries I had connected with more closely during my internship played a role in my receiving the offer. Only two of the actuarial interns received an offer, and I was one of them. Seemingly, everything was aligning in my favor.

By the time I was about to graduate, I had received all of the awards in the math department. Few in the history of that department had ever received as many awards. I also graduated summa cum laude, with highest honors. DePaul had set me on the right path to success with a great start, and I had made promises concerning my career that I intended to keep. All eyes were on me. Everyone believed I would become a great Fellow Actuary and be used to change my world.

I was off to what seemed a great start. Unrecognizable to me at the time was a ticking time bomb ready to explode called "the pressure to perform."

LallyInsurance was located about an hour and a half from where I lived. I chose to stay close to the DePaul campus since my friends and family were still living in that area. I did not want to isolate myself by living far away in the suburbs. However, I did not realize how much of a burden commuting daily to work would be. I commuted by train and bus nearly three hours daily, if not more, but I planned to use that time to study for my actuarial exams.

I saw that the actuaries working at that company were extremely sharp and competitive. Many of them had already passed three to four exams before graduating. I had passed two but was determined to pass more within a year. The reality of full-time work life hit me quickly. I was added to a team working on actuarial valuation, which entailed estimating the company's liabilities (i.e., the amount required to pay the insurance benefits promised). At the start of every month, quarter, or year, we had to ensure that our books were properly closed with proper estimates of the value of our future financial obligations.

I had wanted to work with Thierry on the ALM team, but job openings on that team were usually scarce and competitive. Since the company had a rotation program, I eventually planned to rotate to that team. I was confident that Thierry would ultimately add me to his team. Many in the company knew the actuarial valuation team I had joined routinely worked many extra hours, a fact I did not know when I accepted the position. No one warned me, but I didn't have a choice as to which team I would work with first. I would be on that team for two years until I could rotate out.

I was concerned about the extra work hours on that team because I still had to study and pass actuarial exams. Usually, companies that offer an actuarial program ensure that students take study time during work hours in addition to their personal study time so that they can succeed on their exams. I had planned to take my third four-hour-long actuarial exam, Models for Financial Economics (MFE). I knew I would need to study close to 400 study hours to pass that exam. I made my study plan, which my manager and Thierry reviewed. The only caveat my manager had was that work would take priority over studying if we needed to meet a deadline, but I would be able to catch up during downtime. I quickly realized the issue was that we had very few downtimes on our team. Work was back-to-back and given that I was new and still had much to learn, using any study time at work became almost impossible. All I could rely on was my own personal study time.

I started by studying at home from seven o'clock in the evening and staying up until midnight. I planned to review my notes during my train commute. My plan worked fine at the beginning, but then work got busy. I started staying late at work, and by the time I got on the train or arrived home, I was too exhausted to study.

As a new employee, I was too fearful to explain my situation with my manager. My struggle to balance work and taking exams became so overwhelming, I went to Thierry for some tips. We met in the cafeteria for lunch, and he told me he had good news to share. During our lunch, I told Thierry about my struggle with studying and that I did not think I would be ready to pass the exam that fall with the way my work and study time were in conflict. I was also excited to meet with him because he knew so much and had spent time teaching me about his line of work.

He offered me some advice, such as better organizing my work and communicating with my team. "Be bold and speak to your manager if you feel overworked or have questions." Then he told me his good news. "I will be returning to France with my family. I will be leaving the company early the next year."

Interestingly, I only now thought about the reality that people often switched jobs. In my mind, I had thought I would work with Thierry forever in that company. I was crushed when he told me he was leaving a couple of months after I joined the company. I did my best not to show him my disappointment. I had hoped to switch to his team eventually, and the support he gave me as a mentor had been significant. Coming right off DePaul, I was used to having a solid support team, and the thought that I would be left to figure things out on my own scared me.

What made things worse was that not long after Thierry told me he was leaving, I discovered that Allen was no longer with his company because he could not pass his third actuarial exam. Studying and passing those exams was another reality most actuaries faced while working. We are expected to study for the actuarial exam while we work until we become qualified actuaries, at the very least, associate actuaries.

Most actuarial programs have policies regarding exam performance, including consequences for repeatedly failing an exam. The reason is that each company's actuarial programs invest significant time and resources into training their employees to become qualified actuaries. As a result, new actuarial graduates like me were expected to perform well on exams. Repeatedly failing exams was seen as needing more aptitude or commitment to succeed as an actuary. Termination was a last resort for many companies, including mine, and could become my reality if I repeatedly failed exams. This reality had played out for Allen, and consequently, he had been fired from his company's actuarial program though he never shared that news with me. Someone in the Math Club who had contacted his company told me. The timing of this bad news could not have been worse. Thierry's leaving and my struggling to study for my third exam left me terrified at the idea of what had happened to Allen would happen to me.

I followed Thierry's advice and shared my struggles with my manager. For a couple of weeks, he did his best to readjust my schedule and work so that I could take some study time. My commute had become extremely tiring, and I would often not have the energy to study on the train but would sleep instead. As the time for me to take my third exam came closer, I was only halfway through my study material, and I knew I would fail.

Full-time work was a reality that hit me pretty hard, and I desperately needed to prepare for the test. By the time Thierry left the company, I felt isolated and didn't know who to talk to about my struggles. I was not as close to other actuaries to share with them what I was experiencing. When the exam results were posted, I was devastated to see I had scored a 0 out of 10 on my exam. *How can I share these results with my manager?*

Given my record of always overachieving, receiving a zero was unbearable. I failed, and I had failed terribly.

Even Mom could not console me on the phone. I cried for days over my exam result. For me, the heartbreak was not merely about failing the exam; rather, I was fearful of being unable to pass any more exams and being inadequate to become an actuary. I was terrified of what my future would look like if I did not succeed as an actuary. I was embarrassed that I could not perform as I had set many expectations for myself. I was too ashamed to seek help because I was afraid of being judged for underperforming. Finding out that other actuaries had passed their exams was terrifying because I felt something was wrong with me, causing me to further disconnect from other actuaries. I was ashamed to discuss how badly I was doing while other actuaries in other departments were thriving. No longer being a local champion wasn't easy to accept.

Four key factors affected me in that season of my life. First, during my college years, I had devised a plan with a huge pressure to perform. I was a local champion at DePaul, the highest-achieving student in the math department, always excelling academically. I could not meet the expectations of a new job where the pressure to perform well and meet deadlines while passing actuarial exams was overwhelming.

Second, I knew I needed to learn to communicate well in a work setting. During my internship, the projects I was given were fairly simple compared to the workload I had while working full-time. I was so used to always performing well with a minimum amount of guidance in school that I was afraid to ask questions at work, fearful of appearing inadequate. I was not close to my manager and felt he would only understand me if I asked him a few questions. Consequently, I was left alone to solve situations on my own. Because I wanted to impress, I worked extra hours to resolve the problem on my own rather than ask questions.

Third, I was frustrated by the quantity of work I was assigned, knowing that I still had to study for my exam. I felt I was set up to fail, which greatly frustrated me. I could not study at work or outside of work because of being overworked and exhausted physically. I was also gaining too much weight as I compensated for the stress by overeating.

Fourth, I felt more isolated when Thierry left and Allen disappeared from my life. I was not assigned a mentor and was too afraid to reach out to anyone for fear that they would report what I had said to my manager. Feeling so disconnected only added to my feelings of being alone. I was struggling but did not know who to go to. My years as an overachiever at DePaul were now haunting me at work. I could not perform or keep the high standard I had set for myself.

After failing my actuarial exam, I became very anxious and depressed over my work conditions and started a bad habit I had left long behind in France—smoking cigarettes. I never knew something I had flirted with at the age of seven would make me an addict later in life. I smoked to cope with the stress of work, having to study for an exam under complex conditions, commuting for too long, not liking the type of work I was doing, and feeling that I was a failure and would never become a Fellow Actuary.

I started doubting myself and my abilities to become an actuary. I had to pass three more exams to become an Associate Actuary and three additional ones to become a Fellow Actuary. I could not even get a decent grade on the third one, so I didn't know how on earth I would finish them all. I felt isolated by my inability to deliver and perform well.

I started calling my mom daily on my way back from work to share with her my daily frustration. She generally gave me the same message: "Persevere, Sonya. This is a season of learning how to cope with difficulties. You are so used to achieving perfect results that you get frustrated at the first sign of a setback. Continue to work hard and do not give up on your plans to pass your exam."

Her encouragement gave me new strength to develop a new study schedule for my second attempt at the exam. But what I needed to know and was about to discover was that the actuarial valuation team's first few months of the year would be hectic as we worked on closing the books for the previous year. I soon learned that I would be expected to come to work on Saturdays to ensure we worked cohesively to meet our corporate deadlines. I immediately knew that I would fail my actuarial exam a second time, and I could see no way around this crazy work schedule. When I discussed my struggles with my manager, I was told to "figure it out using my personal study time."

The answer annoyed me, given that work was now infringing on my weekends—the only time I had to study. I just swallowed my frustration.

My cigarette consumption increased to a dangerous level, as I sometimes smoked a whole pack of cigarettes in a day. I was stressed and frustrated, and I hated my job passionately. I was slowly losing my sense of purpose, and instead of persevering, I started to fall back into my old ways. I had a small group of college "acquaintances" who I knew loved to party like there was no tomorrow over weekends. Usually, I would not join them because of schoolwork and actuarial exam study, but during that difficult season of my life, I started associating with them more often.

After long work hours, I found comfort in smoking and drinking heavily. I could no longer take the pressure. I needed an avenue to let it all out, and being with this group of friends was my way of forgetting the troubles I was experiencing at work. I also started finding comfort in food. I started eating junk food instead of cooking meals at home. I felt that I never had time for anything. Work was haunting me, and every time I had a break, I wanted to let it out by drinking and smoking. Communicating my frustrations at work was not something I had been trained to do. I did not want anyone to think my complaints were due to my inability to perform well. I didn't want to look like a failure.

One morning, I took a taxi to work at five in the morning, hoping to arrive early enough to kickstart the monthly valuation process. I wanted show my team I could perform well. I planned to leave early that day to return to the city to study for my exam. Upon arriving at work, I followed all the steps I meticulously documented to kickstart the valuation process assigned to me. Running the models before I could get the correct valuation for review to send to my manager and then the accounting team would take me a couple of hours. By the time my manager arrived at nine o'clock, I had completed a massive chunk of the work. He was quite excited to see that the process was somehow moving ahead.

By eleven o'clock, we sent our numbers to the accounting team. Since we were off to a great start, my plan of arriving early seemed to have worked well for me. However, at two o'clock in the afternoon, we received an email from one of our team members stating that he had made an error and that we needed to rerun our models. He let accounting know we would send updated numbers later in the day.

I was so crushed because I felt I had come early to work for no reason. Not only did we have to rerun everything, but I would also end up staying even later at work. Out of frustration, I rushed to my manager's office to tell him I could not stay late as I had to study for my exam and had already come early to work. He understood my frustration and thanked me for how hard I was working. Nevertheless, he stressed, "What's important here is for our team to deliver the numbers on time so that we can complete the process. Therefore, work takes priority over exams, but you can catch up later."

What I wanted to say but did not know how was: "You want me to pass exams so I can maintain my job. How can I if you do not allow me time to study?"

I was fuming inside and too afraid to speak up to anyone. I felt trapped and that I was being set up for failure. I was already falling behind in my studying again, and, at this point, I was ready to quit.

I stayed in the office until eleven o'clock that night, trying to determine what went wrong. *What did I miss that delayed the process? Was it my fault?*

I called Mom in tears. She had gotten used to my calling her in tears over the past few months. "Mom, I cannot do this any longer. The environment has become too toxic for me to achieve anything."

For the first time, my mother did not know how to advise me. She had never been in that situation, and she was becoming more concerned about my well-being than anything else. She saw the toll work was taking on me. I knew I would fail that exam a second time. I could not bear the idea of failing it again a third time and being fired.

The real world outside of school was nothing like I had imagined, and I did not know how to navigate my circumstances. I did not reach out to anyone because I was too ashamed to seek help; I felt that I had failed everyone. That day at work was the tipping point for me. I no longer wanted to attain my goals if what I was experiencing was what it took to become an Actuary. Never in a million years had I remotely thought that I would reach this point.

By the time the exam came around, we were not as busy at work, but I had fallen so far behind that I could not catch up. I did my best to memorize it all, but I knew passing these exams required much more work than simply memorizing flash cards. On exam day, I felt that I had performed worse than the last time I took that exam. I knew that I had failed the exam again.

The idea of facing my team with a failing score and feeling I would become a laughingstock was unbearable. When I returned to work after my exam, the expectations were the same and kept piling up. In tears again, I called my mom before leaving work that day and told her what I never thought I would ever say. "Mom, it's over. Tomorrow, I am giving them my resignation letter."

After only nine months, I resigned from what I had thought should have been my dream job. I had gained over 30 pounds, had become addicted to cigarettes, and was on the verge of becoming an alcoholic. I was self-destructing with trying to perform and not disappoint anyone. I honestly did not know who to blame but myself. I could not communicate my struggles at work and was left to bear the consequences. I was depressed and had lost hope of ever becoming a Fellow Actuary.

My mom knew that the decision I had made was tough and that I was very depressed. "Sonya, come back to France to rest and rebuild for a couple of months. Figure out what you want to do next. Use that time to study for your actuarial exam full-time instead of working. Passing that third exam will increase your chances of getting a better job."

I liked her suggestion, thinking that hiding in France was a great idea because I didn't want anyone to know I had quit my "dream" job and had failed to keep my promises. I no longer thought that I had it in me to become a Fellow Actuary. I told my manager and team I was returning to France because I missed home. I did not tell them why I had decided to quit. I wanted to leave with what little dignity I had left.

Before leaving for France, I called Sanja, who had become my best friend in college. We had spent hours studying together at the library or nights at her place. We would often talk about our future and how successful we would be in our careers. Through our volunteering with SMILE, she knew I was also passionate about becoming a role model for Black youth and inspiring them to pursue STEM careers. We agreed to meet for coffee by the DePaul campus. I had not told anyone but my family that I had quit my job, but I knew I could tell Sanja without feeling judgment.

I arrived at the coffee shop to reserve a seat for us and saw Sanja through the window waving at me from afar. When I saw her, a wave of tears filled to my eyes. My relationship with Sanja had been filled with hopes as to who we would become in society. At that moment, I felt that I had failed her too. As she sat down, she immediately knew something was terribly wrong. I was so hurt and broken that composing my words took some time. I finally told her, "I could not do it. I feel like a complete failure, and I have been very depressed for months that I will never become an Actuary."

Sanja was so touched that she cried as well. She knew my arriving at such a conclusion must have been heartbreaking for me. "Sonya, I cannot believe how broken you are."

We had not met in person for over six months, and the last time she had seen me, I was still doing fine, adjusting to my new normal. She could not believe how badly the job situation had deteriorated so quickly. "I will be returning to France for two months to determine what to do next. I am not interested in finding a new job immediately. I need a break from my work stress."

Sanja was a Christian, and she replied, "I will pray for you. Is it okay for me to pray for you right now?"

I agreed—though I was not interested in God or religion. However, I realized that I had gotten to such a bad place that I would take anything I could—including a prayer. She touched my heart as she prayed that God would restore my past failures and redeem what I had lost. She also prayed that I would return to the U.S. and not abandon my dreams. I felt a sense of peace after she prayed for me and thanked her for being such a fantastic friend.

———

Mom welcomed me home to France with the most delicious heartwarming meal. She knew I needed to refuel my exhausted body. She kept reminding me how proud she was of me and that a little setback would not cancel my dreams. "Sonya, taking a break to learn from what happened is vital. Take notes on what you could have done better and plan to move forward." Mom did her best to comfort and encourage me over that first meal.

I knew life had thrown an abundance of punches at Mom—not just the horrible incident that happened to her while living on the South Side of Chicago. Mom had learned how to overcome obstacles, and nothing scared her. She had learned how to move ahead in the hard times and desired to impart in me that same fighting spirit.

During that week, I took daily walks around our neighborhood. My mom had bought a house not far from L'abbaye. I started walking around, trying to find purpose and meaning in my life. Mom did not know I was smoking, and I would take walks to smoke and think as I walked around the neighborhood. I passed by my old building at L'abbaye and saw some of the places where I hung out with my rebellious clique— the mall where I was arrested...I walked wherever, trying to make sense of what had happened to me.

I was still quite depressed, but something inside of me kept telling me that I could not give up the fight. *I have come too far to give it all up.* Every time I thought of my actuarial career, I began to weep. Coping with the fact that I had failed was so difficult—at least that is what I thought.

I sat down with Mom a couple of days later, and she asked, "How do you want to proceed? If you want, I'll be your accountability partner. You cannot stay in that state of depression. Why don't you try going to the BnF library? I believe it might help you focus again like you did in high school when you were studying for the BAC."

I took my laptop, where I had saved my exam study manual, and went to the library the next day. Mom was right; going to the BnF enabled me to return to where I dreamt with Aria and Adrian in high school. I had gone to the BnF when I had to redeem myself from my rebellious years to ensure that I passed the BAC. By going to BnF, I could pick myself up a little from the heavy cloud of depression I was in.

After a few days of returning to the BnF, I began studying in earnest for my third actuarial exam again. Seeing other students there gave me a boost as well to keep moving forward. I developed a study plan to enable me to study for two actuarial exams that summer. I wanted to maximize my time since I was not working. I planned to take both exams in the fall, but the exams would be two weeks apart. The fourth exam, "Construction and Evaluation of Actuarial Models" (Exam C), was a four-hour exam covering survival models and statistical distributions. For me, being able to pass both exams would be like revenge for the shame I felt I had endured.

I went to the library in the morning, studied for a couple of hours, stopped to eat and smoke for an hour, then return to studying for a couple of hours before returning home. My smoking habit did not diminish in France; if anything, the smoking was a way to cope with the shame and anxiety I constantly felt. I was diligent throughout the summer, focusing on passing these exams. With time, I found hope again to return to being an Actuary.

I registered to take my actuarial exams in France during the fall. As the dates of the exams were approaching, I was becoming more and more nervous. I was close to covering all the study material and needed to work as many practice problems as possible. The third exam was now a computer-based exam so the results would be displayed on the computer right after I completed the exam. Exam C was the same way.

I would not have to wait two months for the results as usual. I was at a point where I could no longer take another failure. I was extremely fragile, and I would frequently break down for no reason.

I studied hard that summer and gave my studies all I had. At that point, failing these exams would mean I was not fit to become an Actuary. Taking these two tests was my last try for my actuarial career.

The place to take both exams was in the Louvre area of Paris. I arrived on both days nearly two hours ahead of time. I wanted to ensure I was as relaxed as possible. I did not eat on the day of each exam, but I made sure to smoke my daily cigarette quota to help alleviate my stress. I took my third exam MFE first on a Wednesday. The Prometric exam room was freezing, but I had worn a warm jacket and socks.

I was very nervous and shaking before clicking on the page to start my exam. Then my stomach started to hurt. If my state of mind continued like this, I would need to go to the bathroom and lose precious exam time. When I finally started, I knew immediately that I was too nervous to complete it correctly. The first question was tricky, and I could not get the multiple-answer choices to match what I had. I really panicked as my mind screamed, *what if I fail again?*"

Then the weirdest thought came to my mind. I felt the need to pray like Sanja had done for me before leaving Chicago. Praying was not something I had ever done myself, but somehow I decided to. I stopped what I was doing and closed my eyes. I said in my heart: "Please, God, if You are real, help me. I studied and did the best I could, but now I am going to need You to help me pass this exam. If You don't show up, I will fail it because I am too stressed."

By the time I opened my eyes, I felt the same peace I felt after Sanja had prayed for me. The overwhelming anxiety had left me. I continued with my exam questions. This was the most challenging exam of the last two I had already taken. The questions were seemingly becoming more challenging each time I failed and had to retake the exam. However, I had studied well and knew how to answer most of the questions.

When I completed the exam, I was prompted to the page that told me that I was about to get a preliminary exam pass or fail result. All I had to do was click "Next." I took a very deep breath, put the cursor on the "Next" button, closed my eyes, and clicked. The first thing I saw when I opened my eyes was "Congratulations...." I immediately burst into tears.

Relief, joy, and peace flooded my being. I ran out of the exam center and called my parents. I was so happy, I was screaming for joy and crying at the same time. I walked for almost 30 minutes, smiling and reflecting on what had happened before I could get to a train station to return home.

I took exam C, my fourth actuarial exam, precisely two weeks later. I faced this exam in the same way. I was not as anxious as I was at the last exam, but I still said the same prayer, asking for God's help. In my mind, I began thinking that maybe God was real after all.

When I finished the exam, I took a deep breath, put the cursor on the "Next" button, closed my eyes, and clicked. When I opened my eyes, I had to catch myself to keep from screaming. I had passed that exam as well.

Again, I sprinted outside and called my parents in tears. To my mom, I said, "Mom, you were right. Maybe I am called to be an Actuary after all."

I could see the light again. I was dreaming again. Going to France partially helped me to restore myself and remember how far I had come. As Sanja had prayed, I had gained the strength to return to the United States. With four actuarial exams passed, I planned to apply for a new actuarial job and get back on the train to become a Fellow Actuary.

Chapter 8

But God Picked Me Up!

————

I returned to the States after staying in France for nearly nine months. France had become like a hideout for me where I did not need to face my classmates or professors to explain why I had failed at my last job. With four actuarial exams in the bag, I was confident that any employer would hire me as I was only one exam away from earning my actuarial Associateship. Employers preferred actuarial employees who had a higher chance of getting certified, given that insurance companies need certified actuaries to sign official documents.

I immediately started applying for work upon my arrival. My goal was to focus on companies in downtown Chicago so that I would not have to worry about commuting or isolating myself in a distant location away from my family. I was too fragile and not in a state where I could live alone. I stayed with my younger sister, who lived in a tiny studio apartment in downtown Chicago. She was completing her Ph.D. at the University of Chicago and allowed me to stay with her until I could settle myself financially. I no longer had any savings. If only I had been more financially responsible when working at LallyInsurance. Instead, I had wasted a lot of money on food, partying, and taking taxis back to the city whenever I did not feel like taking the train. I had to find a job quickly so that I would not become a burden to anyone.

The year 2011 was a challenging one for many job seekers. The recession caused many businesses to cut costs and reduce their workforce, leading to high levels of unemployment and fierce competition for available jobs. About 60 percent of recent graduates could not obtain a full-time job in their chosen profession. I was about to find out the hard way. I applied to all of the entry-level jobs available in Chicago and was able to get an interview with a consulting firm located in downtown Chicago. I was assured that their exam program was not as rigid as LallyInsurance. I would not be required to take exams during the busy season. I was so close to becoming an Associate Actuary, and I knew at that point, most companies do not force actuaries to get their Fellowship if they do not want to. So, I faced a low probability that what had happened at LallyInsurance could ever happen to me again. On the interview day, I arrived early, and I was very confident.

I had applied for an entry-level actuarial role. That level of work only required passing two actuarial exams. I had nearly a year of experience, including my actuarial internship, so I felt good about my outcome of getting the role. I also knew a lot about that organization and the type of consulting work they did. Two actuarial analysts and one director interviewed me. The interviews with the actuarial analysts went very well, and I could answer the technical questions they asked me in Excel. I also asked thoughtful questions about how the economy affected their work dynamic. I got a lot of smiles and positive head nodding from them.

The director I interviewed with immediately greeted me with a smile as if he knew me from somewhere. I had told the recruiter that I had just returned from France, where I had taken a short sabbatical. The director was curious about what I had been doing during that time, and I told him that I had studied for exams and had taken the time to restore myself.

He was impressed that I had passed two actuarial exams so close to each other. Then he asked me the one question that I believe blew up the interview. "Why did you leave your last position so quickly?"

I told him that actuarial valuation work was different from the type of work that interested me. "I want to do more actuarial modeling work, and the long commute to the office had become too cumbersome. I prefer a role closer to my family."

My answer was genuine and reasonable, but I did not know that this director was a close friend of my former boss. Right after I answered his question, he announced, "I know your former manager very well. I have plans to catch up with him soon." His plans did not bother me because I had given him honest answers. However, my answer was different from what I had told my former boss. I had told him before leaving LallyInsurance that I was returning to France. I was too afraid to tell him the real reason why I was quitting.

Interestingly, I have to wonder if the director conducting the interview had already talked to my former boss about me, and my answers were not quite what he had expected. I never heard back from that team, and for the following six months, I kept applying for all types of actuarial and finance-related roles, but I could not get an interview.

In the meantime, a couple of friends and I decided to work on a tech startup company in hopes that it would grow while we worked full-time. We planned to build a website application to connect entrepreneurs to investors, and sell multiple services online. We all knew our startup would take time to develop and would not bring in any revenue until we launched, and we would need time to gain some real traction. Given that I was still mourning my actuarial career and what it could have been, my heart was not entirely in the startup when we started it. The job began as a hideout for my past failures and so I could tell people I was doing something when they asked me. However, the startup launch dragged on for so long that I even became embarrassed to mention it. Nothing seemed to be working in my life.

I became highly demoralized again. The little hope surging after passing my last two actuarial exams was gone. I was back to a place of total depression. I felt like a failure in my family and that the cards had flipped entirely against me. I was the university celebrity with the perfect future set for her, and I felt like I had destroyed all my chances of a great career. I was too ashamed to reach out to anyone. How would I explain to them why I had quit my first job? They would blame me for making such a mistake, especially during a recession. I blamed myself for not sticking with the role, even if it was difficult. The tremendous load of guilt I carried made me feel unredeemable. No matter what I did, I could not become an actuary. The worse part was that I felt as if everyone was doing well but me.

Most of my classmates at DePaul had secured full-time jobs, and I blamed myself for not working as hard as they had to keep their jobs. Financially, I felt like a burden to my family. My sister loaned me money to take care of some personal needs and let me stay in her place for free. However, I always felt so much embarrassment and shame whenever her friends asked her why I was around. My self-worth and self-esteem had tanked. I was emotionally, financially, and mentally depressed. I had let down my parents, who had worked hard to see their children succeed in their careers. I had disappointed everyone who believed in me. Smoking was the only way I felt I had to help me cope. I had smoked so much that I had come to hate the habit, but I could not stop. I had become an addict and dependent on a cigarette to release the anxiety and shame I felt daily. Not being able to get a job started to impact my mental health seriously. I was so down that I could not think of other career options. I was stuck in that bubble of having failed at LallyInsurance.

One day, after getting another rejection email, I reached my breaking point. I was in my sister's apartment alone and on my knees. I felt so hopeless having nothing to be proud of, and for the first time in my life, I started having suicidal thoughts. I started looking back at my life and agonized over how I had destroyed so many opportunities, starting with missing out on attending a Grande École in France because of my rebellious behavior in high school and now being jobless because I could not perform at work and gave it all up. I also did not like who I had become as a person. I was angry at my situation and at others, and smoking cigarettes was slowly killing me daily. Feeling constantly consumed by guilt made me hate my life. So, on my knees, I did what I thought would be my last hope at some redemption by crying out to God.

Jesus, if You are real like Sanja told me, I need You to show up right now. I don't like my life anymore and have made so many mistakes. I am ashamed of myself, and I can't get anything right. If You are real, please deliver me from this misery and pick me up. I surrender what is left of me to You. I don't have any other hope. Please, show me a way out; otherwise, I don't want to live this life anymore.

For the third time in my life, I cried out to God for help. I had not believed in God nor did I care about His existence, but my circumstances had finally humbled me. Sanja had been preaching to me and taking me to her church to encourage me, but I was still adamant about God or religion. Yet, when life humbled me, and I had no one to rescue me from my mental agony, my only thought was to cry out to God. After all, He did show up the two other times I had called on Him during my actuarial exams. Just like I had felt that immense peace after Sanja had prayed for me and when I prayed, I felt a huge sense of peace and clarity. All I knew was that I felt so much peace that instead of worrying, I fell asleep.

When I woke up the following morning, I knew something had shifted. I went to bed as a cigarette addict and woke up with total disgust for cigarettes. I usually smoked in the morning, but that morning the mere thought of smoking disgusted me and I threw away my last pack of cigarettes. When I eventually went outside, someone smoking passed me, and again, I felt that same overwhelming disgust. I usually wanted to smoke right after smelling cigarettes or after a meal, but I no longer felt the urge. I knew God had answered my prayers, and my overnight aversion to cigarettes was His sign to show me that He had heard my prayer.

Truly, a miracle had happened: I was no longer addicted to cigarettes. I knew on that day that God was real; Jesus was real. No one had convinced me of such, I prayed on my own, and He answered in a way that I could not deny His existence. I called Sanja and told her what had happened and that I believed Jesus was real. She cried on the phone and said, "Jesus loves you, and He is about to turn your whole life around for your good! You will no longer remember the shame of your past."

Sanja was right! Everything about my life changed for the better from that point on. Sanja encouraged me to go to church to learn more about Jesus and His amazing plans for my life. I began attending a church called Jesus House Chicago (JHC), a Nigerian-based church in Chicago. JHC was the community my parents looked for but unfortunately never found when they moved to the United States in the late 1990s. My parents did not have mentors to whom they could open up about their struggles and who could have helped them navigate the job market in the United States. Of course, not having mentors contributed to Mom's eventual return to France.

JHC was the place I needed to be in at that point in my life. The church was not only full of successful African-immigrant professionals with whom I could easily relate but was also a place where I began to build my identity apart from my career. JHC was the community that helped me come out of the depression. I started finding joy in life aside from my career by attending JHC. Up until that point, my career had defined my self-worth and self-esteem.

I enjoyed going to JHC because I felt so much positivity and life in that church. Every week I attended their service, I left with a joy that made me come back for more. The worship music and message from the pastor and ministers were uplifting me week by week. Messages of hope encouraging me to push forward and not give up. We sang songs of hope that God would turn around even the worst situations for my good. Above all, I learned that my worth had nothing to do with my career success but with how much God loved me despite my imperfections.

Though I was currently jobless, I found hope by knowing that I was not a failure and that my future would be amazing because God's hand was on my life. I was still worthy, and my struggles were temporary and would surely make me stronger. I no longer needed the praise of people to validate me. I no longer wanted to impress a boss, a professor, a coworker, or a classmate. God loved me despite what I could bring to the table, and I was now rebuilding my self-confidence in Him. Going to JHC was one of the main reasons I stopped being depressed. I filled my life with so much hope in that church that the cloud of sadness was removed. I started to hope and dream again.

I remained without a full-time job for the following two years after joining JHC. Jesus didn't magically bring a job immediately into my life. I believed He allowed me to walk into what I called my "season of wilderness." During that time, I worked on the startup, which had since launched and had gained some traction but still needed to generate revenue. So, I had to hustle to bring in income while hoping for either the startup to raise investor funds to be able to pay me or hoping that I would get a more stable job. I secured multiple tutoring clients and a part-time secretarial job that did not pay much but was enough to keep me going for the time being. My sister continued to graciously allow me to stay with her, and she found a larger studio so we could live together more comfortably.

I thought about taking my fifth actuarial exam, but I had become discouraged over the job search that I was not even sure I would be able to get an actuarial job again. That exam was known to be one of the most challenging of the actuarial exams, and to me, without an actuarial job it didn't make sense to take more exams. So, I decided to put taking any more actuarial exams on pause.

The DePaul library became my official office, where I would meet with clients to review their math and actuarial problems and hold online meetings with my startup team. This season of my life was humbling, and I truly believe God allowed me to go through it because I had become too full of myself. I had lived off the praise and validation of people far too long. I cared too much about what people thought of me, which is why I ran away at first sight of failure in my career. I feared what others would think of me. I believe God needed to teach me this lesson so I would not repeat the same mistake.

Dr. Karina caught me one day by the DePaul library. I had not returned to the math department even though I frequently visited the campus. Maybe I still felt ashamed of my situation. Dr. Karina was so excited to see me and asked me if I was studying for my fellowship exam since I was near the library. I knew that time would come when my professors discovered I was not currently working as an actuary, and I needed to accept that reality. I was learning to no longer live in shame, which was my test.

"Dr. Karina, I am working at a startup while looking for new actuarial work. I left my actuarial job as it was not a good fit for me."

I could see by her shocked expression that she was disapointed. I was no longer the successful student she had hoped I would be. I realized that my character was being formed through moments like meeting Dr.

Karina. Not having much to show her was a humbling moment. I knew God was somehow delivering me from the praises of others.

I learned to be at peace in my situation that I knew was only temporary. God would eventually show up with something much better for me. These times were not always easy, and I had to encourage myself whenever circumstances served to remind me of my past.

One such moment happened when I saw some of my former classmates receive promotions at work or become Associate or Fellow Actuaries. I was happy for them, but their advancement somehow made me feel like I had missed out on something. Nevertheless, I learned that my life journey was personal and unique. I was not in a race with other people. God was making me the best version of myself—not someone who would be competing with others. I did not need to compare myself to anyone. We all have our times and seasons, and I did not need to envy anyone. My time would eventually come, and, in the meantime, I had to celebrate others when their time for increase came.

I am so thankful when looking back at those years in the wilderness when I seemed to be a nobody to everybody. I learned to detach myself from the perceived judgment of others and accept myself for the journey I was on. I learned to be resilient and not let adversity break me down into depression. I learned to pick myself up whenever circumstances wanted to make me believe I was a failure. I stopped self-destructing to overcome life's challenges—a negative pattern in my "past" life.

As a child, I hated being home because my parents were not often there, and the adventures outside the home exposed me to dangers that haunted me years later. As a teenager, I struggled to find my identity seeing my family's struggles and what I thought was injustice toward people who looked like me. I was on the path of delinquency, which led to my police arrest, and I almost destroyed my future career outcomes. Later as a working professional, I almost self-destructed as I smoked my life away.

Thank God, I was learning to unlearn from these self-destructive tendencies. I surrendered to the One Who helped and guided me, giving me the strength to fight life's adversity correctly—with resilience and faith.

My identity was no longer in anyone's validation of me or a job, but in the immense love Jesus had for me and demonstrated by saving me from myself. I became a better and much stronger version of myself. Jesus picked me up from a depression that almost killed me. To Him be ALL the glory!

The startup did not work out as we had hoped, and I knew I would not have a future in it. In only a matter of time after its launch, we closed the business. Investors were not interested in sowing money into it despite how much we had worked to prove that our web application could gain more traction with time. I prayed for God to show me my next career move, given that I thought I was no longer marketable as an actuary. God answered me through the guidance of a mentor.

On a particular Sunday, right after church had ended, a woman minister, Pastor DTO, had been noticing me for some time, and she felt she needed to connect with me. She waved at me after the service and asked me to join her in her office for a talk. I poured out my heart to her about the last years of my life, sharing some of my mistakes, and that I was coming out of that depression. Pastor DTO encouraged me and told me not to worry about anything that might have happened in the past. "I am confident things will get better for you, Sonya. There are no problematic situations that God cannot turn around for your good."

She also gave me some advice as to how I could move forward in my career. Pastor DTO was a successful accountant turned pastor who had previously worked at one of the top accounting firms. She was very familiar with the corporate world and how a person could market herself.

―――――――――――

"My identity was no longer in anyone's validation of me or a job, but in the immense love Jesus had for me and demonstrated by saving me from myself."

―――――――――――

She encouraged me to maximize my time by completing a certificate or a degree to get additional skills to make myself more marketable. She told me not to be so focused on actuarial careers but assess what other related careers were gaining traction in which I could earn a certificate in.

I would not have agreed to that idea years ago since my eyes were only on becoming an actuary. However, I was now open to different career options. I saw Pastor DTO's guidance as a great idea that would enable me to bridge the gap I had on my résumé. As my depression lifted, my mind became clearer. I was finally able to leave behind my past. With the support and accountability I was getting at JHC and from my family, I regained the strength to invest time and energy toward my future career plans.

My sister had heard about a new education platform called Coursera that had just launched with multiple certificates available at low prices. She planned to take additional statistics learning courses to support her Ph.D. thesis and encouraged me to look into it. When I eventually looked into Coursera, I found that the company had a scholarship program to help pay for an entire certificate program that could be used to get jobs, and I qualified for that scholarship. I was immediately interested.

In particular, Coursera was launching its first Data Science Certificate with John Hopkins University, and many people were enrolling in it. What caught my attention was that I could learn computer programming languages like Python and SQL that would be very marketable. While applying for roles in the past, I had seen a greater demand for these skills. I knew earning this certification would be a great use of my time. I planned to reapply for full-time jobs once I obtained my certificate.

When I eventually started this program, I learned that data science was booming in the marketplace, including areas in which actuaries work. Data science started to gain significant popularity around 2012-2013, and by 2014 had become a highly sought-after profession. The availability of large datasets, advancements in machine learning algorithms, and the growth of cloud computing infrastructure were some of the key factors contributing to data science's rise as a marketable skill.

When I started the Data Science program in the late fall of 2014, the timing was perfect. The skills I gained through that program positioned me well in the marketplace. I didn't know that when I was starting, so I am confident that God's hand was moving in my favor, positioning me in the best place for my career.

Although our startup had not generated income, I could apply what I was learning in my Data Science program using that startup data. I gained practical experience that I could use to build my résumé. Above all, I was gaining skills that would set me apart as an actuary. More specifically, I learned how to extract insights from large, complex data and identify trends that could help actuaries make informed decisions. I learned about machine learning and how to build predictive models beyond the traditional model actuaries used to make more accurate predictions about future outcomes or events. I learned how to automate many of the tasks that actuaries traditionally performed manually, which would save time and money for companies and reduce errors. I also learned how to visualize complex data and present findings in a way that would be easy for management to understand and make informed decisions.

I was learning so much and gaining ground as a professional. The projects I completed in my data science program could be used during my interviews to demonstrate my technical abilities. My interview pitch was that I could extract insights from vast data and develop predictive models to help companies manage risks more effectively. Risk management was the core of actuarial work, and with my newfound skills, I could maximize how actuaries do their work. That Data Science certificate was heaven-sent to make up for the years of wilderness in my life. I completed my Data Science certificate with distinction, and recruiters were already contacting me. A divine shift was happening in my life. I was again excited about my future and knew the perfect work opportunity would soon open for me.

"The blessing of the Lord brings wealth, without painful toil for it." - Proverbs 10:22 (NIV)

I was terrified of having another work experience similar to what I had endured at LallyInsurance. I had prayed for a long time that God would bless me with a career that would bring joy and peace into my life—not cause anxiety and fear. I was willing to work hard and learn but not at the expense of my mental health. This time, I was setting rules for what a company needed to deliver for me. I did not need to prove myself; I knew what I was bringing to the table. I needed to set some boundaries within my career to keep myself sane.

I stood on the promise of Proverbs 10:22 that God would bless me with a job that would make me rich but not add sorrow to my life. That is precisely the favor that happened to me with the actuarial job I eventually got. I started applying for work as soon as my Data Science program ended with the goal of merging data science into my actuarial career. I had worked so hard to study for my actuarial exams, and I had a strong leading that I had something valuable for the actuarial profession. I knew actuarial roles would come with exam support so that I could continue taking exams and get back on track to become a certified actuary.

I started looking for insurance companies, which were the familiar places where actuaries worked, either looking for actuaries with data science-related skills or with an established data science department in which I could potentially work. Many health insurance companies were building data science capabilities at the time, so I started educating myself about health insurance and how my skills could benefit such companies. My years at the startup had at least helped me learn how to pitch myself well, given that we pitched our project to investors for years. I had gained a multitude of marketing skills.

I found one particular company in the heart of downtown Chicago, HealthBlue, that was building a data science department to tackle significant healthcare challenges. HealthBlue already had an established actuarial department working with various company areas. This company would be a great fit because I could work as an actuary and later request to rotate into the new data science department.

HealthBlue had a particular actuarial opening that fitted my profile perfectly. The available Associate role required at least four actuarial exams and one year of actuarial work experience. I had taken four actuarial exams, and with my internship and full-time work at LallyInsurance, I had exactly one year of actuarial work experience. I honestly thought God created the role for me. I applied and was contacted by a recruiter almost immediately. What a massive change from the constant rejection I used to experience when applying for actuarial work! I was so excited. I read everything I could find about that company and the type of work they did. I read articles about challenges actuaries should prepare to face in the future in healthcare, and I had many questions I was prepared to ask those I would interview. I knew God's hand was on this job, and in my mind, I could not see how I would mess up this opportunity.

I knew I was ready for that job when I woke up on the interview day. The commute to that office was very smooth and quick due to its central location, so I knew that if I worked there, I would have time for the people with whom I do life outside of work. I went to the interview with the mindset of a winner—not someone desperate.

When my family had moved to Chicago when I was a child, I

remember seeing one particular skyscraper at the heart of downtown Chicago that I always thought would be like a dream if I worked there. To my surprise, HealthBlue was located in the building next door, and HealthBlue's skyscraper was ten times more beautiful than that white one I had thought was amazing. Working in a skyscraper was the image of what the American dream had looked like to my family 20 years earlier, and now I was interviewing in one of them!

The view of downtown Chicago and Lake Michigan was breathtaking from the building. Just the thought of going to work there daily was like therapy. I was so excited about this job opportunity. I interviewed on a Wednesday, and the sky was bright blue despite being cold outside. I arrived 30 minutes early, and I stood by one of the building pillars, placed my hand there, and offered a simple prayer of peace and favor. I needed everything to align to favor me. My day was off to a fantastic start.

My day was very long, but I persevered through meeting with eight different actuaries who tested my technical and soft skills. SQL was a highly sought skill in that company. I was well versed in SQL, given that I had learned it during my data science training, so I felt good about that part of the interview process. I also met with a director I checked out on LinkedIn and learned she worked on Medicare product pricing. I had spent significant time reading about the healthcare environment in that product line, so we had a rich conversation on that topic. She could see that I had put a great deal of effort into preparing for the interview. As I pitched my plans to use my data science skills to enhance the work in the company, I could tell she was quite enthused with my ideas.

The last person I met with was a vice president, and I knew I needed to make a good impression on him. During my discussion with him, I discovered that he led the Actuarial Valuation department of the company and expressed his interest in having me join his team, given my background of working in an actuarial valuation team.

I had grown out of being a people pleaser and was determined to set healthy boundaries in my work. I said, "I would prefer another actuarial rotation to learn something new, but I am flexible as long as the role offers work-life balance." I told him about my expectations regarding work-life balance to assess whether the company overworked its employees. I had been traumatized about my experience at LallyInsurance. I could not afford working at a company that did not value balance. I wanted him to know that I would not be working on weekends or consistently long hours, but would only do so when I had to take personal study time for actuarial exams during exam season. He needed to see that I valued balance in my life.

My mental health had become tremendously important to me over the past few years, and I was no longer willing to sacrifice it for a job. I had learned my lesson. When he asked about my salary expectation, I gave him a range based on my one year of actuarial experience and three years of tech startup experience I had. I could tell he was surprised by how assertive I was about my competencies and expectations.

"Your salary expectation is above what the company has in mind for this role, but I will see what I can do because we like your profile."

The interview had gone exactly as I had wanted. I had set the right tone for what I could bring to them and what I was expecting in return. I was determined to have a new job that would not come with painful toil attached.

I received an email from the recruiter that following Friday asking when she could call. I immediately responded, telling her she could call anytime. She called then and gave me the news I had waited for almost four years. "We are extending an offer for you to join our company as an Actuarial Associate." The salary was precisely within the range I had requested. *The Vice President's honoring my request was a good sign.* When I hung up the phone, I screamed at the top of my lungs! I was so relieved to know that my years of labor in my actuarial career and even working on that startup would not be in vain. Everything I labored on was finally seen as valuable for a role.

I felt my years in the wilderness had somehow been redeemed. I called my parents to share the good news. How happy and excited they were for me! They had been on this actuarial train with me from the beginning—through all the tears and the joy.

"I am not surprised. I knew that a door would open for you to return to be an actuary," Mom said.

I knew Mom had always believed in my ability to become an actuary despite my challenges. "Sonya, meditate on the lessons you have learned over the past few years and do not lose hold of them at this new workplace. I am so proud of who you are becoming, and I'm so thankful that you have come out of that wilderness season victoriously."

The joy I felt that day was beyond imaginable and describable. I felt like a dream had come true. I spent the rest of the weekend planning my move into my apartment I would finally be able to afford. A new season was beginning for me.

I was placed on the Medicare pricing team when I started working at HealthBlue. My manager was a young Caucasian man, only a couple of years older than me. Allan had a very calming voice and would always smile during conversations. I had a good feeling about him from the beginning. Allan and I became close almost from the onset. Allan took me to lunch my first week of work to get to know me better. During our lunch, we talked about our hobbies and families. His family played an essential part in his life; we definitely had that in common. Allan also loved to travel and was fascinated by my cultural background. I learned he was also a data enthusiast and found interest in the data science training I had completed. We shared several common interests.

Allan told me early on that he wanted me to be successful at passing actuarial exams and encouraged me to form a study plan early to start preparing for my fifth actuarial exam. I was amazed by how much he wanted to support my exam success as I did not have the best experience in the past with management supporting that journey. Allan gave me a lot of time to phase in and adjust to my new role. He did not rush me into completing new tasks but wanted me to have the proper foundation to succeed in my role.

I found Allan to be a very balanced employee, and I was thankful he was my manager. He would rarely stay late at work. He valued his family time, needing to be home at a reasonable time to be with his family. I had prayed that I would have the actuarial job I always dreamt of while doing the things I always wanted to do outside of work. Allan shared the same vision for life, and I knew that job would be a blessing to me. HealthBlue was the perfect addition to my life. Working for the company redeemed the years I felt I had failed as an actuary. I could finally look back at the past and laugh.

Over the next few months at HealthBlue, Allan became a mentor in my career. He believed in my ability to succeed as an actuary and cheered me on in my exams and learning journey on the job. He set the proper structure so I could excel at work and on my exams. He saw my success as his success as my manager. Everything he felt could benefit me, he shared with me. He spent a lot of time ensuring I understood what our work entailed and that I had the necessary training to excel at it. Allan also made certain that I took all the study time I had available to take at work.

He never bluntly told me work took priority over exams. Instead, he created a balance so I could excel at both. Allan shaped my view of what a great actuarial manager looked like. From the start, Allan set me up for great success within the company and as an actuary. Allan was my confirmation that I had landed in the right place. HealthBlue was an answer to my long-awaited prayers. I had no doubt in my mind that God's hand was on that job. Everything was aligning for me into pleasant places. God picked me up and fully redeemed my years of tears, regrets, and shame.

For God so loved the world that he gave his one and only Son, that whoever believes in him shall not perish but have eternal life. – John 3:16 (NIV)

Faith is very personal, and I fully respect your decision regarding your beliefs. I felt sharing my own journey that led to my faith in Jesus Christ was an important part of my story. Having faith in Him literally saved my life and played the major role in my being where I am now in my career. I cried to Jesus in my brokenness and yielded my heart to Him, and He showed up so powerfully to help me. That is how much Jesus loves you and me!

Chapter 9

The Final Stretch to Becoming a Fellow Actuary

———————

I became an Associate of the Society of Actuary (ASA) in December 2017. I had completed all the requirements for my associateship within a year of joining HealthBlue. The company was setting me up on the right track for success in my career. I was blossoming, but I wanted to be done with actuarial exams. I was not yet a Fellow Actuary, but I was officially a credentialed Actuary. My company did not require me to continue to the fellowship level if being a Fellow was no part of my plan. Of all the credentialed Actuaries within the Society of Actuaries, only half had achieved their Fellowship.

I did not feel like I had it in me to continue and take three more long actuarial exams. I had taken my first actuarial exam ten years earlier as a sophomore, and the journey to where I was had been long with many bumps and roadblocks. I had finally achieved part of my dream to become a credentialed Actuary. Working under Allan, I was also thriving. Having a manager who was invested in my success as a professional showed in my work. He had also promoted me to the Senior Associate level as I had balanced my work performance well while taking my actuarial exam. This season of my life was full of blessings. I had also met the love of my life, and I finally felt that I was living the balanced life I dreamt of and reaching many of the goals I set for myself.

I met with my pastor at JHC to share some of the great things happening in my career. I recall the day I came to his office four years prior in tears, telling him that I was very broke and broken. I had no money left in the bank. He had signed a check and handed it to me, ensuring I would be cared for until I could get on my feet. Over time, he became like a father to me, regularly checking to see how I was progressing personally and professionally. He was excited to see how great things had turned out for me and that I was reaching many of my career goals.

When I met with him, without even knowing that there was a higher level beyond associateship, my pastor impressed on me the importance of pushing beyond where I was at as an Actuary and going to the highest level of education in my career. His encouragement was one of the things I loved about JHC; our pastor believed that Christians needed to be examples in the workplace and demonstrate that there were no limits when we put our faith in God to achieve big things.

Successful professionals surrounded me at JHC, and my pastor expected nothing less from me. I thanked him for his advice but made sure not to mention that Fellowship was a higher level to attain in my career. In the back of my mind, I was not yet thoroughly convinced I could continue with the time-consuming actuarial exams. I had always felt like I was missing out on doing other fun things while studying. I was in love and wanted to use my time to build what would be my future family life, and I did not want the sacrifice required to pass actuarial exams to get in the way of my relationship.

Overall, I was living the life my parents could be proud of, which was worth their sacrifice. I was at peace with where I was in my career, but I knew I needed to face a particular reality in the workplace. I knew I had made a commitment in years past that I now needed to keep. I was comfortable where I was, but I knew something in particular wasn't sitting right within me about what I had noticed over the years at HealthBlue.

I had been working in the company for nearly two years now and was also part of the recruiting team. I was seeing an area in the company that became more and more of a burden, especially during large town hall meetings filled with actuaries working for the company. I was the *only* Black Actuary within HealthBlue—one of the largest health insurance companies employing well over 100 actuaries. Something within me was not at rest with that fact. I had become so comfortable making personal strides that I was forgetting about my commitment I had made years earlier. I believed that I was meant to be an Actuary for a bigger purpose than myself, and I needed to reconnect with the vision I had to diversify my profession.

Even while being part of the actuarial recruiting team, I had never seen a Black candidate come in person to interview. I do not believe HealthBlue was intentionally not hiring Black actuaries. I knew the environment in my company was not hostile to minorities. On the contrary, I not only felt HealthBlue was the perfect environment for minorities to thrive but leaders within the organization believed diversity was essential to the company's success.

As a Black Actuary, I felt included and supported within the company. I never felt discriminated against. Our recruiting process seemed fair, competitive and unbiased—at least from the many interviews I had been a part of. The main issue was that the pipeline for Black talent was extremely scarce within the actuarial profession. According to the 2018 US Actuarial Diversity and Inclusion Report published by the Actuarial Foundation, the percentage of Black or African American actuaries in the United States was 3.1 percent, an extremely low representation compared to the overall U.S. population, with Black or African Americans comprising around 13.4 percent.

I was becoming increasingly convicted for not doing anything about changing those statistics. In the past I had been so passionate about investing efforts toward diversifying STEM careers. My years in the wilderness, as I liked to call them, had made me forget some of the bigger goals I had promised to reach. My first couple of years at HealthBlue had been focused on securing my role by not failing exams. Now that I was a credentialed Actuary, I needed to invest more time to revive my passion. *Purpose was calling.*

After one of our actuarial town hall meetings, I stopped our Chief Actuary and told her I wanted to start an initiative within the actuarial department to diversify our talent pipeline. HealthBlue was already very committed to DEI (Diversity, Equity, and Inclusion), and every department had a goal to commit to DEI initiatives. The Chief Actuary was thrilled that I wanted to lead diversity efforts and admitted that the actuarial department had fallen behind on implementing these initiatives. She told me to make a proposal with options and action plans and report to her when I was ready. I wasted no time and started my outreach.

My starting point was the International Association of Black Actuaries (IABA). I last connected with the IABA when I worked at LallyInsurance six years earlier. After Allan left the profession, I never reconnected with the organization. At the time, the IABA was still growing, and little did I know that I was about to be blown away by how much growth had occurred over the years within the organization. I emailed the IABA's Executive Director to schedule a meeting to see how HealthBlue could partner with the IABA to diversify our talent pipeline. When I eventually met with her, she explained that the IABA had almost tripled in size since the last time I had attended their annual meeting.

"Many companies are competing for IABA's top talents. DEI is at the forefront of many organizations, spending top dollars on sponsorship packages for IABA meetings to get the first pick at IABA top actuarial talent. May I suggest that your company attend the upcoming annual

IABA meeting, our largest conference scheduled in two months. You can get a sponsorship package that will enable your company to interview candidates at the event."

She continued to explain that some companies were flying a considerable part of their actuarial recruiting team to interview candidates at the IABA annual meeting and were even extending job offers on the spot. Hearing how some companies partnered with the IABA to increase their diversity pipeline was inspiring. I desperately wanted HealthBlue to join those ranks.

The second outreach was to historically Black colleges and universities (HBCUs). I searched online and collected the emails of actuarial or math department chairs of all the HBCUs in the United States. I sent them individual emails to introduce myself and HealthBlue, as well as to inquire how HealthBlue could partner with their institution to channel actuarial talent. Most schools responded, but only a few had either an actuarial program or students interested in actuarial science.

Only two universities were interested in discussing more, but only one had a big enough class size for us to invest time and effort. At the time, Morgan State University (MSU) was the only HBCU with an actuarial program. I scheduled a call with the MSU Actuarial Director. She explained the dynamics of their actuarial program and what she believed would be the best way for our company to connect with her students. She proposed that our team travel to their campus to meet the actuarial students in her actuarial capstone class, which would allow us to introduce our company to students and collect their résumés. Coming in person would also demonstrate our commitment to the school and its students.

My third outreach was to HealthBlue's internal DEI Team. I wanted to be sure I leveraged internal resources to support this new diversity initiative within the actuarial department. I connected with the DEI lead at HealthBlue to explain what I had noticed and what I was trying to achieve. He confirmed that their team was aware of the lack of diversity within particular departments due to the talent pipeline needing to be more diverse. He immediately jumped on board with the options I was planning to propose to the Chief Actuary and shared with me the ways HealthBlue DEI team could support, more specifically, our university outreach. I was excited as I had gathered many great options that I would report back to the Chief Actuary.

Since we were already very close to the IABA meeting, the Chief Actuary agreed to sponsor me to attend the conference and proposed that I schedule an internal group meeting with the different internal stakeholders I had met to agree on our best steps forward. The goal was to attend the IABA meeting to network as much as I could and gather information to assess what kind of sponsorship package would best fit HealthBlue in the future. I was excited to see my company's commitment to diversifying the actuarial talent pipeline. The leadership was fully supportive of my vision.

Attending the IABA meeting after years of hiatus from the organization was incredibly humbling. The truth was that I felt a little ashamed of myself when I saw how much growth had occurred within the IABA since my last attendance and that I had played no role in that expansion. I knew I had let down the organization, and many who believed I would be vested in diversifying the profession. I recognized faces from the last time I attended; many now played a significant role at the conference. I almost wanted to hide as I saw companies with booths and actuarial professionals everywhere. *God forbid someone's asking me where I had been.*

Nevertheless, I walked in, making myself low, observing how amazing the event was and how well IABA had done over the years. As I was about to exit the registration area to start networking in hopes of collecting résumés, one of the attendees stopped me. He introduced himself as Robert, mentioning that he was Cameroonian and had recognized my last name as also being of Cameroonian-descent. "Is this your first time at the conference?"

I responded that I had attended in the past, but it had been a long time since I had connected with the IABA. I could tell that my response shocked him and felt that he almost wanted to say, "You have missed out!"

He was right; I had missed out on a lot.

In my years of struggling at LallyInsurance and trying to get a job later, the IABA could have helped me, but I isolated myself instead of reaching out and seeking help. The IABA had become a significant resource for Black Actuaries in the industry. Robert told me that all the actuaries he had mentored through IABA and who attended the annual meeting secured jobs. He also shared that a large group of Cameroonian-descent was attending the IABA. They had formed a sub-group within the IABA to network with each other and assess how they could support students in North America and Cameroon. He asked me if I wanted to join their table and the meeting they would have the next day. I immediately agreed and felt so thankful that I was reconnecting with the IABA.

The next day was the famous IABA Awards banquet, the magical banquet that made me dream about becoming a Fellow Actuary. I attended this same awards banquet while in college and saw for the first time how Black Actuaries were celebrated within the IABA for becoming Associates and Fellows. The banquet had been one of the major events that inspired me to become a Fellow Actuary one day.

I had planned not to attend the banquet that day. During the registration process, I had put down that I was a new Associate Actuary, and I knew that my name would be called if I attended the banquet. The issue was that I had disconnected from the IABA and knew no one within the organization besides the IABA executive director with whom I had briefly spoken. I was embarrassed by the fact that I had done nothing to contribute to the IABA, and I didn't want to expose myself. In my mind, no one would clap for me.

However, Robert and many of the other Cameroonian actuaries in attendance convinced me that I had no reason to feel badly and that I had been given a fresh start to renew my commitment. When I arrived at the awards banquet, the Cameroonian Actuaries had reserved three tables for their group, and to my surprise, they had reserved a seat for me. I truly felt honored and so thankful for them all. I saw my name on the pamphlet of those who are new Associates and was apprehensive when it would come time to call my name forward for my award. I was terrified at people I had met years past thinking, *Where has she been?*

The awards ceremony started with calling forth the new Associate Actuaries. I could hear people clapping and saw standing ovations for the new Associates. When my name was eventually called, to my pleasant surprise, all of the Cameroonian Actuaries stood and shouted and clapped for me. An onlooker would have thought I had my family in the room. Seeing me, a Black woman of Cameroonian-descent become a credentialed Actuary meant so much to them, and their support touched me.

When I sat down, one of the Cameroonian Actuaries, who was already a Fellow Actuary, sitting next to me, congratulated me, and asked, "You know what's next?" He then answered his question for me and said, "It is important that you continue the journey to get your Fellowship. Do not give up! We need to shift the statistics."

He impressed on me the importance of thinking about the next generation. I was not only doing it for myself but to motivate others too. "Other young women will be inspired by seeing you reach the top of your career. More specifically, we can inspire many Black students both here in the United States and abroad to dream higher without limit. If more and more of us Black actuaries reached the top of our careers, those who follow us would not even see that height as something hard to reach. They will have already seen themselves in us at the top!"

The combination of how they had celebrated me and what this Cameroonian Fellow Actuary said moved me. I felt so compelled to push higher. A fire within me had been re-ignited to inspire and support other minorities to become Fellow Actuaries.

I returned to HealthBlue with a fresh fire, putting what I saw at the IABA meeting into action. To make our diversity initiatives more formal, I formed a committee within the actuarial department, including all the internal stakeholders with whom I had already spoken. I summarized with them the different options to get involved within the IABA and MSU. I also added the option of getting involved with the Organization Latino Actuaries (OLA). I was on fire and on a mission; the Chief Actuary and everyone on that committee could tell. I especially wanted to make sure that HealthBlue fully understood that I was not asking the company to lower its recruiting standard. Rather, my goal was to find top minority talent as competent as other actuaries in the company, if not more. I did not identify issues in our recruitment process, which I believe was thorough to ensure merit was achieved to get any role. The actuarial exam requirement was helpful in establishing that requisite since they were all standardized. We would not be giving handouts to anyone; rather, anyone who got a role at HealthBlue would know he or she worked hard for it and deserved it. My mom always thought me that "only hard work pays off" and I wanted to uphold this standard to give everyone the opportunity to prove themselves.

I was raised to believe that hard work was the only route to success, and I had no plans to change that example my parents had successfully set. The goal of our diversity initiative was to increase the number of resumes we collect and ensure that these resumes represented an "as much diverse" talent pool as we could get with reasonable efforts. I spent the next few months executing the diversity initiatives we agreed on and studying for my first fellowship exam.

When I started studying for my first fellowship exam, I told myself that if I passed on the first try, it truly meant that I was supposed to become a Fellow Actuary, and I would persevere on. I was not sure I would continue if I started by failing. The first two Fellowship exams were 4 to 5 hours long and would require me to study an average of 400 to 500 hours to pass these rigorous exams. I was horrified at the idea of studying that much and still failing.

The first exam, Group and Health Core, tested my knowledge of group and health insurance, including pricing, underwriting, reserving, and risk management. I formed an aggressive study plan upon returning from the IABA meeting, which consisted of studying past work hours on weekdays and all day on weekends. I took a break on Sunday morning so I could attend church. I also had to inform my boyfriend and explain why we could not spend as much time together.

Only actuarial students could fully understand the commitment required for these exams. What motivated me from the beginning was that I was not only doing it for the financial benefit, even though that would be significant as Fellow Actuaries, on average, made more money than Associate Actuaries. What truly motivated me and drove me to study was that I was doing it for something bigger than myself. I was pushing the limits to inspire other minorities so they would no longer see getting their Fellowship as a limitation. My main inspiration kept me studying intensely for that first fellowship exam. With the support of my work team, my family, my church, and my boyfriend, I made it to exam day fully prepared.

———————————

"I was pushing the limits to inspire other minorities so they would no longer see getting their Fellowship as a limitation. "

———————————

I walked from my house to the exam location, which was interestingly located at the DePaul University downtown campus. Everything was coming back full circle. I felt as if I was meant to take that exam. Something was significant about my taking it there since DePaul was where my actuarial journey had started.

The walk took me about 30 minutes, and as I walked, I kept confessing and declaring that I would be successful at the exam, and I kept speaking positively about what my exam experience would be like. I actually had a paper I had created at the start of studying for my exam on which I had my name, exam number, the exam date, and the logo of the Society of Actuaries. I added to that paper in bold that I had passed that particular fellowship exam, which was my way of activating my faith. Every day until that exam date, I spoke over that paper (vision board) that what was written on it would eventually come to pass.

I had built my faith and put in the work to back it up. I was prepared mentally and physically. Like I had done before, I started the exam with a prayer. I felt no anxiety or fear and started the exam with a clear mind. The exam was challenging, containing problems I had never tackled while studying, but I had developed an exam strategy that enabled me to overcome the fear of failing. Fellowship exams were mainly written exams, not the multiple-choice format of Associateship exams. My plan was clear. I would answer every question to the best of my ability and focus only on questions I knew I could solve correctly. I would not waste extra time on problems I knew I could not solve fully but instead quickly write my best guess as an answer.

That strategy paid off as I was able to complete the exam while many others struggled to finish, having spent too much time on the difficult part of the exam. When we were done, I felt good about my exam, but I had no idea how well I would perform. Exam results usually came two months after the exam, which was the norm for most actuarial exams. I would usually study during that time in case I had failed so that I could keep everything I had memorized in my brain, but I did not feel the need to do this for that exam. In the back of my mind, I had the thought that if I had failed, especially after giving it my all, it meant Fellowship exams were not for me.

I was still at home the day the Fellowship exam results were posted. Since they were usually posted on a Friday around nine o'clock in the morning, I planned to head to the office after the exam results. If I failed, I would at least be able to digest the news privately before going to the office. I was on the phone with Mom when the time came to check my result.

Things happened so quickly that I can barely remember what I clicked on my laptop. All I knew was that I had my candidate number memorized, and I needed to check whether it appeared on the list of passing candidates. Immediately as I opened the list of passing candidate numbers for my Fellowship exam, I saw my number right in front of my eyes. I screamed at the top of my lungs. "Mom, I can hardly believe it; I passed! Now I am stuck; I have to pass them all!"

On the following Monday, when the exam grades were released, I saw, to my surprise, that I had scored a 9 out of 10. I was shocked because I had never attained a score greater than 8! My score meant that I had it in me to become a Fellow Actuary and that the journey to my Fellowship would be smoother than I had thought. My score was my confirmation that I needed to press forward.

My work was truly aligning in my favor. I had, along with a coworker on my team who was as passionate as me about applying data science to our actuarial work area, created a data science subgroup. Our goal was to gather data science enthusiasts across the company to discuss applications of data science on practical work projects. HealthBlue had formed its data science department shortly after I had joined, and the vice president in charge was an Actuary. To our pleasant surprise, he joined our first data science sub-group meeting. He was very impressed by our presentation and discussion. I had never met him but had only discussed with him via the group.

HealthBlue's actuarial rotational program was designed to provide actuaries with exposure to various actuarial functions within an organization. Our rotational program shifted actuaries on average every two years. I was up for rotation, and I had selected an advanced analytical team as my top option. The data science department did not have an actuarial rotation opening so I could not select to join that team. Most actuaries were not exposed to data science at the time, so for an actuary to work within that data science department would have required a great learning curve.

I learned behind the scenes that the vice president leading the data science team created an actuarial rotation opening for me to join their data science team. He had been impressed with my involvement in the data science subgroup and requested that I be transferred to his team. I could not believe it when Allan told me. Joining that team was precisely what I had hoped before joining HealthBlue and was a direct answer to my prayers. Everything at HealthBlue was aligning to favor me.

James, my new manager within the data science department, was part African American and was a former actuary turned data scientist. He was very familiar with the IABA, and we connected from the beginning as we shared many commonalities. Coming into this new team, I was actually nervous about whether I would be supported the same way Allan had supported me. I was thriving under Allan, and I had prayed that the same favor would follow me into my new department. Thank God, it did! James was beyond amazing. He was more than a manager and a mentor. He became an advocate for my career and each of the endeavors I was pursuing at HealthBlue. From the beginning of working under him, he started supporting and advocating for the work I was doing to diversify the actuarial talent pipeline within the company.

I was not even on an actuarial team, so he had no real benefit in supporting me. He could have seen it as a distraction to focusing on my new role within his team. However, such was not the case; James saw how important it was for me to pursue this passion, and he trusted I would still perform well at work while leading this initiative. James was also very supportive of my continuing my fellowship exams and told me that he would ensure that I used all of my work study time so that I would be successful. I was in such a healthy and supportive environment that I had no other choice but to thrive, and I did.

On a personal level, I had gotten engaged right before joining the data science team, and we were planning to get married the following year. It was summertime, and I did not want to put my fiancé through the stress of seeing me study for another actuarial exam. I wanted to be able to enjoy the summer with him and spend time planning our wedding. So, I told James I would delay my next Fellowship exam until after my wedding. I planned to use that gap year to put in extra time to learn and dig deep into the data science projects my team was working on. I also wanted to use the extra time to refresh some of the skills I had gained in my data science certificate program, such as Python programming and machine learning models.

I was very invested in hosting and leading the company data science subgroup, using it as a platform to apply what I was learning on the team. That time enabled me to become an asset to my team more quickly as I learned and participated in new projects. James was very pleased with my performance, and to my surprise, he promoted me to the managerial level only six months after being on his team. Not long after being promoted, James put me in charge of an imitative that would save our company millions of dollars if executed successfully.

I had to start from scratch, building a predictive model to help our company cut Emergency Room (ER) costs while working collaboratively with our network of medical providers. James felt I would be a perfect fit for this new project given my unique skills at understanding how to interpret health data as an actuary via my experience and actuarial exams, and ability to manipulate large datasets through my data science training. I was excited about this project from the beginning, but I had no idea how great of a success this project would end up being.

I officially married the love of my life in May 2019. Holistically, my life had flipped entirely from my years in the wilderness and depression. I felt like I was becoming the best version of myself. Personally, and professionally, I was achieving goals beyond my expectations. Having a supportive environment was a critical factor in my being able to succeed. When someone is surrounded by people who believe in them, provide encouragement and support, and offer constructive feedback, a positive and empowering atmosphere is created that fosters growth and development. I was surrounded by people who loved and believed in me. The workplace culture I was in was committed to my development. I was also part of a fantastic church community that supported me when I was at the lowest point of my life and invested so much love and time in my personal development.

Not long after our honeymoon, I got back on the actuarial exam train. My second fellowship exam, Group and Health Advanced exam, was also a five-hour long exam, requiring a significant amount of time away from home. That exam tested my knowledge of more advanced group and health insurance topics, such as financial reporting, product development, and enterprise risk management. My study strategy was to go after work to the DePaul library, a 15-minute walk from our apartment. I would stay there for at least three hours daily after work but planned on staying even longer when I got closer to the exam date. I also planned to study on Saturday afternoon after taking care of things around the house, and Sunday afternoon after church. This exam was tough for me to tackle, and I would sometimes stay past midnight at the library.

I felt a lot of pressure, especially now that I was married. I did not want to be selfish by not putting my all into passing that exam. I did not want to put my husband through years and years of cycles of passing and failing exams. I studied my heart out to guarantee that each time I studied, I would pass the exam. I only had two remaining, and I was determined to pass them on the first try.

To avoid my having to take taxis home daily, my husband started walking to the library to meet me so we could return home together. Since we lived in the middle of the city, we did not have a car. He took it upon himself to go above and beyond to show that he was with me while I was studying. He faithfully met me daily at midnight at the library for almost three months. He knew that this would motivate me, and we would usually have a great time walking back home together or going to eat late at night.

Because of that exam's difficulty level, I was less confident in how I would perform compared to the first fellowship exam I took. At work, James gave me additional days off before my exam to study without even needing to take PTOs. James wanted to see me succeed, and he knew how much effort I was already putting in at work. James wanted to see me become a Fellow Actuary.

The exam day was long; we had both the morning and afternoon sessions. I had memorized hundreds of notecards, and I was really exhausted. I could not wait to be done with the exam. The morning session seemed easier to me than the afternoon session. I made a major error solving a problem in the afternoon session, so I was unsure if I could pass. My faith was more shaken with that exam given that I had more at stake. I did not want actuarial exams to interfere with my marriage.

Nevertheless, I gave my best on that exam day and knew I would at least get a break for the next few months. My husband and I traveled to celebrate, having sacrificed so much over the past few months.

On the day my exam results were released, I asked my husband to stay behind in case I failed the exam. I knew I would need his emotional support. I planned to get to work that Friday later in the morning. However, I got so anxious at home that I asked my husband to walk me to the bus stop instead and that I would check the exam score while we were outside so I would not feel confined at home. He did his best to help me relax and kept reminding me of how hard I had worked and that was what mattered most.

I had given my best, and regardless of the result, I needed to be proud of myself. I felt better that he was willing to forgive me for putting him through all the stress of an exam without passing it. As he walked me to my bus stop, I was all over the place. I could not stay still until nine o'clock came.

We had crossed the street that led to the bus stop, and I turned to tell him that it was time to check my exam results. I had no idea that my husband had in mind to film my reaction as he already felt that I had most likely passed it. He wanted to capture the joy of that moment. So, I took my phone, quickly went to the Society of Actuaries Exam Result page, and again looked for my exam number. Fewer candidates had passed this Fellowship exam than the first one I took, so I was worried. I looked through that short list of passing candidates, and finally saw my candidate numbers for the morning and afternoon exam sessions. I had passed both sections of the exam on the first try!

I screamed, cried, and laughed, all at the same time. My husband recorded every bit of that joyous moment, and I was truly grateful he did. When I got to work, I also told James the good news, and he was so excited that he organized a team lunch to celebrate with me. Here I was, now two-thirds of the way to becoming a Fellow Actuary. *I am getting closer and closer to the finish line!*

At work, the project James had given me to lead was gaining more traction. My team had grown, and five people were now working on it. What was so exciting was that through that project, I had the opportunity to develop and market a new product that our team had built from scratch. It was exactly what I had done in years past in the unsuccessful startup, but that experience gained was the foundation of the work I was now doing on my team. I found a lot of passion in my work and the bigger mission I was a part of.

HealthBlue had officially partnered with the IABA and MSU and made significant investments in these organizations. I had become an official actuarial mentor within and outside of the IABA, and I was doing my best to inspire younger minority actuaries. Our partnership with MSU was so successful that the actuarial director invited me to join their actuarial board. I also put together a Python training course that I gave for MSU summer actuarial program. I was investing in what I had promised to do and truly felt called to do. I was inspiring the next generation of Black actuaries and taking bold steps to break the barriers before them. One of those barriers was passing my last Fellowship exam.

The two-hour Group and Health Specialty actuarial fellowship exam covered topics such as disease management, health provider reimbursement, and employee benefits strategy. This two-hour-long exam gave the illusion of being easier, but that misconception was far from the truth! The exam covered over 400 hours of study material, but candidates would only be tested on half of it. I could spend hours and hours on topics that would not appear on the exam. I had no idea which specific sections to choose to cut study time given that I would most likely fail if the test included a topic I did not study.

Once again, I created a study plan and formed a strategy to ensure success. The study plan was similar to what I had already formulated. I would sacrifice precious time to be away from home at the library. I started studying at the end of January, and the exam would take place in May. I started on a good note and really enjoyed what I was learning. That Fellowship exam was my favorite. I could personally relate to the study material as my data science team worked closely with value-based care providers, which was an exam topic. I understood how some of the topics were applied at work. After only over a month of studying, two major news hit our family.

The first was COVID-19, which happened in the middle of my intense studying for my last exam. I remember coming to work that week, and James recommended to the entire team that we stay home for the rest of the week. I was so focused on my exam that I had not taken the time to research much about what was happening. My husband gave me the major rundown concerning the expanding COVID cases.

I will never forget March 16, 2020, when the mayor of Chicago announced that the city would be on lockdown starting the next day. Interestingly, right before the mayor's announcement, I took a home pregnancy test and discovered I was expecting. The announcement was bittersweet for our family as we were rejoicing over what our future would be as a family but also worried about how COVID would impact our lives, as well as the lives of many.

Studying during the lockdown became extremely difficult almost from the beginning. I started having morning sickness and being confined at home seemed to exacerbate my symptoms. I could not handle the smell of anything and everything. Studying became almost impossible as I would often be exhausted after working, but thankfully, the Society of Actuaries announced that the exam would be postponed to July. I decided to use that extra time to pause my exam studying until I felt better.

Nearly two months passed before I came to a place where I could pick up studying more intensely, but at that time, I only had two months left before my exam. I was unsure of what to do and was conflicted about whether to take the exam. I thought it would not be possible for me to catch up and put in the final studying needed to pass. However, studying while being a new mom was a reality that many had discouraged. Finding study time would be almost impossible as a young mom. So, I was terrified at the possibility of delaying my exam any further. Twelve years had passed since I had taken my first actuarial exam. *I just want to be done and turn the page to a new chapter!* However, I was stuck with time.

My husband encouraged me to try my best and push through. "Don't worry about the chores around the house. All I want you to do is study when you are not at work." Bless his heart, he took care of cleaning, laundry, and cooking. All he wanted me to do was study as much as possible.

My mom called to tell me to use my coming baby as my inspiration and encouragement while studying. "You are doing this for your baby, creating a world where only the sky will be the limit for her."

I thank God because everything aligned for me to study without any distractions and with much emotional support. Even my baby remained healthy and kept her mommy healthy to be in the best shape to pass her exam. Since studying at home could often be distracting, my church allowed me to use their facility to study during the lockdown. Mornings and evenings were a race against the clock. I had never memorized that much in such a short period. Every opportunity I had, I was either memorizing a note card or creating a new one.

The final stages of achieving a goal can sometimes be the most challenging. I was tired, given that mine had been a long journey, and I was terrified at potentially failing so close to the finish line. James also supported me by giving me extra time off to make up for the time I paused studying because I was not feeling well. During that time, my team had made significant strides on our project, and we were beginning to form relationships with key medical executives to promote our product to external partners. James knew I was a hard worker and that, despite my health challenges, I had given my best to see our team succeed. He also knew how important it was for me to pass that exam, so he did not allow work to overwhelm me at the finish line. I felt as if all eyes were on me, and I did not want to fail anyone, including my husband, my baby, my co-workers, my church, and myself. I had to stay focused and resilient until the end.

I arrived on the day of the exam, five months pregnant. My abdomen was already showing, but I had worn an oversized jacket to cover it despite the day's being very sunny. My former manager Allan was also taking that same exam, and I had meant to tell him as a surprise after the exam that I was expecting. The room was well spaced with tables six feet apart due to the COVID rules. I sat toward the front as I did not want to get nervous by seeing another student becoming anxious. Despite the time crunch, I had given it my all, and I had been able to go over all the study material. This time, when I prayed before taking the exam, I said, "Thank You, God, that this will be my last exam; I have faith for it."

To my surprise, I knew how to solve all the questions on the exam because this Fellowship exam was not as complex as the others. The only thing that will differentiate me from other candidates was how in-depth I answered each question based on how much I had memorized. The great thing about taking Fellowship exams was that I had become a flash-card memorization machine. I had taken in so much knowledge in my short-term memory, and I would spill it all up on the exam. That strategy worked well for me, given how in-depth answers were needed. I had memorized copious amounts of material.

I finished the exam feeling confident in my answers, and I didn't want to get anxious over it to prevent stressing my baby. When we were all done, I turned around and greeted Allan and a couple of coworkers who were also taking that same exam. Then I proceeded to remove my jacket with a smile and posed so they could see the good news. They were all excited for me and shocked that I had taken the exam while expecting. I was shocked too but more at the fact that I could overcome the challenges I had faced in the past months and still take the exam.

The exam results came back in early September. If I had passed, I would be officially done with actuarial exams. That feeling alone was great. If I had failed, the next time I would be able to take any exam may have been years down the line. I could not imagine sacrificing precious time in seeing my children grow to take exams. Yet, I was at peace. I knew that what was meant to happen was what would eventually happen. Everything was in God's hands.

I had given my all, and I was at peace with myself. I was extremely relaxed when I went to the Society of Actuaries website that day to see if my candidate number was on the passing list. That list was much shorter than any other exam. The crazy thing was that the passing rate for that exam was the lowest it had been in over six years—44 percent. Yet, despite it all, I saw my candidate number on the list right before my eyes. I could not believe it! I had passed and was forever done studying for actuarial exams! I was so emotional that I cried for joy. I thanked my husband for his support.

He immediately joked, "Do I have my wife back now?"

We laughed because truly actuarial exams had become like another lover, but my husband had showed me so much grace. I also called my parents to tell them the good news. As always, my mom praised my efforts. "I always knew you would get there. I am so proud of you."

I called my dad to thank him for his sacrifices in my life. Dad had always encouraged me to persist with my actuarial exam journey.

I also called Aunt Christine who had introduced me to the actuarial profession. She was ecstatic that I had fulfilled her dream.

At work, James and my team were extremely happy for me, and if it had not been for COVID, they would have organized a lovely gathering for me. I put smiles on the faces of many people that day, and I am forever thankful for my "village" who stood by me through that journey. But above all, I am forever thankful to Jesus for picking me up when I had nowhere else to turn and for turning my life into a testimony.

The Fellowship Admissions Course (FAC) was the last stage to pass after completing all the other Fellowship requirements. This last qualification was much easier than taking Fellowship exams but still had to be taken seriously. The FAC was more centered around ethics and required that we give a presentation. Due to COVID, I was given the option to do the FAC online or wait until the FAC resumed in person in December 2021. Many actuaries attended the in-person FAC because the SOA held an award celebration where the actuaries were officially presented their Fellowship certificates. Usually, we were allowed to bring a couple of family members to the FAC banquet dinner. That moment was when actuaries could collectively cheer each other for a job well done and take pictures with their loved ones.

I wanted my daughter to be there to see how far her mom had achieved. I waited until the in-person FAC to receive my Fellowship designation officially. We flew as a family to a gorgeous hotel where the FAC was held. Unfortunately, due to COVID, my parents could not attend, but I knew their hearts were with me. This was their award as much as mine. My daughter was still a baby, and even though she did not yet understand what was happening, I knew she would be proud that her mother had pushed herself to reach her goals.

Having children brings another meaning to life and puts many things in perspective. I had gone through that Fellowship journey not for myself alone but for my children and the next generations after me. I did it to model to them that if they have faith to believe in themselves despite life challenges and work hard toward their goals, they will achieve everything they set their hearts to do. I had made it! Fifteen years had passed since my coming to the United States to study. I was now officially a Black Fellow of the Society of Actuaries. To God be ALL the glory!

PS: Attending the IABA Banquet Award after reaching my FSA was an event I had prayed for and waited for years. At that very banquet a decade earlier, I had captured the vision of one day becoming a Fellow Actuary. Nevertheless, another miracle was growing and glowing within me when the IABA Annual Meeting occurred for that FSA year—my second child. I chose to stay home with him to ease my pregnancy. The miracle of being presented with my Fellowship Award at the IABA still took place in my heart!

Conclusion

Purpose Is Calling

———————

The senior director of my data science team, the one to whom James reported, scheduled a surprise meeting on my calendar. He sent me a note and told me to be near my work phone on that day and time. He did not give me any information but told me he had good news so I should not worry. I sat waiting on a Wednesday afternoon around three o'clock. When someone called from an unknown number, I picked up the call, and to my surprise, the CEO and president of our company was calling to award me with the President's Diversity and Inclusion Leadership Award. The company honored me with this award in recognition of my leadership involvement in diversifying the talent pipeline in the actuarial department of HealthBlue.

Out of over 20,000 employees, I was the one selected for that award. What made it even more meaningful was that our CEO was an African American male; in fact, the first Black person to become CEO in our company. His success was inspiring many, especially in the Black community. I was honored and thankful for the recognition. More importantly, I wanted him to know that I was counting on his support to multiply the efforts we had already put into the groundwork of the actuarial department. I spoke of the importance for our company to guarantee that we had the right level of representation across all areas of our business. Our company's growth was dependent on our having high-performing and diverse teams.

He was excited to see my passion and encouraged me to continue to add value to my team and the collective work we did as a company to be a model in the marketplace. My involvement in the diversity initiatives we launched in the actuarial department started out of passion. I used my own personal time to craft plans and made sure we executed them. I did it out of passion—not for recognition.

I find it interesting that when we are passionate about something, we will devote time and effort to it. When we do something well, others may take notice and recognize our achievements. I was genuinely passionate and dedicated to what I was doing and despite being busy with work and studying for exams, I knew this cause could not wait until I had more time. What made the recognition rewarding was that I felt supported and thankful that I was part of an organization that valued what I brought to the table and invested in me. This award was not my award alone; rather, the award belonged to a combination of people who had inspired me to multiply myself in others and the people who provided the support needed to see this vision come to pass. I am forever thankful to the leadership at HealthBlue for believing in me as they did.

Anna, a vice president and actuary within HealthBlue, had heard about my recent recognition and reached out to me to learn how she could get involved with our diversity initiatives. Anna was already very involved with the Society of Actuaries in advancing DEI within the profession. I discovered that we both shared a passion for diversifying our profession. We met for coffee, and she was curious to learn more about me and what ignited this passion I had. I shared a little with her about my background as a Black woman in science, always in classrooms or working for companies with few to no minority representation. I knew something was not right and needed to change, especially when growing up in inner cities with a significant minority population with limited access to quality education and job opportunities. God had lifted me so that I could extend my hand to lift others. I was called to shift the statistics of minorities in STEM.

My passion fascinated Anna, and I was inspired to see her encouraging me to press forward. We had a vibrant and purposeful conversation, and the plan was that she would be the midpoint contact to provide support and guidance whenever the Chief Actuary was unavailable to do so. I did not know that Anna had referred me to the Society of Actuary team, thinking my story should be featured in *The Actuary* magazine.

I was contacted a couple of days later by a member of the magazine to see if I would be interested in having my story featured. I agreed to be interviewed because I saw the article as an opportunity for me to publicize the actuarial organizations we supported in the hopes of gaining support from other companies. I had no idea the editors planned for me to be the cover model and for my interview to be the feature article in that edition. Amazing!

While working through editing and correcting the magazine feature, the editors were particularly impressed by my involvement at DePaul in the SMILE program. They wanted to visit San Miguel School's Austin campus, where I had volunteered years past, to take pictures of myself for the magazine feature. Unfortunately, the school had closed in 2012 due to a lack of funding, so the SMILE program no longer existed. That closure happened only two years after I had graduated from DePaul. I had lost contact with the SMILE program director and the amazing kids I was able to mentor there.

As an alternative, the magazine coordinator suggested we take pictures of me at the DePaul campus. On that day, I was so excited to walk the editing team through DePaul and talk a little about my involvement with SMILE at that time of my life. While walking through the campus, I was reliving the joy and fulfillment of investing in these amazing students. I know we had a significant impact on their lives at that time. The photographer took my picture and recorded some of the stories I shared. We parted ways after a long morning preparing for the magazine feature.

I headed to the small coffee shop inside DePaul's science building. I always went to that coffee shop while in college, so it brought great memories of seeing students in that area as it reminded me of the great time I had as a student at DePaul. As I arrived at the register to make my coffee order, I felt I knew who the cashier was but could not fully remember.

As she prepared my drink, I kept staring at her. *I know I knew her from somewhere.* She could see that I was staring at her and smiled. When I asked her name, she said, "Deborah," and it immediately clicked. I asked, "Do you remember me from the SMILE program, I used to tutor you?"

She acknowledged that she remembered the SMILE program and added that it had closed not long after we used to come.

"How are the other students doing? Are you still in contact with them?"

"They are all doing well."

I remembered her well. When she was ten years younger, she had expressed an interest in attending DePaul. "What year are you at DePaul?"

Her answer shook me to the core.

"I am not a student at DePaul; I did not go to college. I am working as a cashier in this coffee shop to make ends meet."

Our meeting did not feel like a coincidence. I was about to be featured for having impacted the educational trajectory of students for the better, including those in the SMILE program, but right then, I felt I had failed Deborah. I could not understand why she never went to college. If she had gone to college, she would be graduating by now. When she was in middle school at San Miguel, our team had spent over two years with her in the SMILE program, inspiring her to seek higher education, and she was even interested then in attending DePaul. Deborah was a very bright student.

"Why don't you want to go to college anymore? You did so well in the SMILE program."

"Life has been tough, but I will think about it again."

I took her number and told her I would love to stay in touch to see if I could mentor her. She gladly shared her contact with me, and I left after giving her a big hug. I had tears in my eyes leaving DePaul that day...

What started as a great day with being featured for my work in my company ended on an interesting note that brought some disappointment. I called Sanja in tears, telling her what had happened. Nothing was wrong with being a cashier, but I truly believed Deborah wanted to pursue higher education when she was younger and most likely lacked support along the way.

Sanja remembered who Deborah was and was also very surprised. Deborah had become one of the top-performing students in the SMILE program, and we would not have expected her to not consider going to college. The reality was that after San Miguel School closed in Austin, the students were placed in a neighboring school, and we wondered if they had received the same level of support they had received at San Miguel.

The San Miguel Schools aimed at enrolling underserved students from low-income families who were falling behind. That program focused on ensuring these students stayed off the streets and received the support they needed to seek higher education. The school had significant budget gaps leading to its closure, and the grand vision they had unfortunately ended. I believe if San Miguel had remained open, Deborah would have most likely gone to college.

So much work still needs to be done was the lesson I learned the day I met Deborah. As much as it is great to be recognized for being a change agent, seeing the change long term is far more fulfilling. Effecting long-term change is my mission.

My heart's passion is for effecting change in inner cities, under-resourced neighborhoods, because I grew up in these communities. Inner cities have higher rates of poverty, crime, and other social issues, which contribute to higher delinquency rates. My mother recognized these risks—the high rates of school dropouts, the limited opportunities for higher education and career advancement, and high youth delinquency rates in our neighborhoods in France and Chicago. She insisted we attend a private school in Paris because of the significant barriers in our neighborhood schools to access to quality education, including underfunded schools, lack of resources, lower-quality teachers, lack of exposure to specific careers such as STEM careers, and limited access to extracurricular activities and programs. My mother understood education plays a crucial role in helping individuals and communities overcome these challenges.

For those very reasons the San Miguel Schools had been planted in neighborhoods like Austin in Chicago. Many of these afterschool programs, such as SMILE, were designed to keep the youth focused on their educational future to overcome some of the significant issues their communities face. Education is a critical factor in the well-being of the future of inner cities youth. Education is what enabled me to escape the path of delinquency.

I believe long-term educational and mentoring programs similar to SMILE should be put in place in inner cities to help address some of the educational gaps students may face. These programs could also be augmented by STEM or fine arts to provide even greater exposure to areas of interest. Such programs should include mentoring, tutoring, and extracurricular activities components to support and inspire students' long-term academic growth from at least middle school until they graduate from college.

Obviously, more than these programs will be needed to solve the broader issues such as poverty, housing, crime or healthcare, which can all significantly impact academic achievement and long-term success. However, such programs can help focus youth on aspiring for higher education. Funding and the work required to implement such programs will be significant. It would require much more effort than we all thought at HealthBlue. The talent pipeline in STEM careers is often not diverse and extremely small due to deeper issues that consequently impact the quality of STEM or even general education in some neighborhoods with large minority populations such as inner cities. Getting proper minority representation in STEM careers would be challenging unless significant holistic efforts are put in place to address these deeply rooted issues. The combined efforts of various organizations would be required, such as foundations, community centers and organizations, policymakers, companies, and local officials, working together to enact changes and enhance the level of STEM education in these under-resourced communities.

Part of my life's calling is to stir interest in these initiatives and potentially become a leader along the way. It will take many generations to see the full potential impact of such work, but I firmly believe that we are all called to make our world a better place for those who will come after us.

I wrote this book to invite you to make a difference in another person's life like many have made a difference in my life. If that police officer had not extended grace to me, I may not have been able to achieve my career goals. I encourage you to look into how you could mentor someone else or think differently about someone you previously looked down on at home, school, work, or community. We don't know what people have been through, so we should not be too quick to judge their

"The combined efforts of various organizations would be required, such as foundations, community centers and organizations, policymakers, companies, and local officials, working together to enact changes and enhance the level of STEM education in these under-resourced communities."

actions. Let's instead extend grace for them to rise higher.

I also wrote this book to invite those who felt they had messed up, as I once did, to take responsibility and learn from their actions. If you are in a depressive state, please seek counseling for mental health guidance. I truly believe God will extend grace to you through people, and better opportunities will eventually come your way. You must take hold of them and rise to the challenge. You are not a failure, and it is never too late for you to change for the better. Your success story could one day inspire someone who traveled the same path as you to rise higher. We are all meant to become the best version of ourselves and multiply our best self in others.

Finally, let me close by saying that God can change anyone for the better and turn the mess of his or her life into a message to inspire others. I am a testimony of such a reality. I rose from a fallen youth on the path of delinquency to becoming a Fellow of the Society of Actuaries, and in so doing, I became a role model for others to follow.

To God be ALL the glory!

Notes

Introduction

1. Neal Templin, "Want to Be an Actuary? Odds Are, You'll Fail the Test," Wall Street Journal, Dec. 28, 2021, https://www.wsj.com/articles/actuary-credential-test-exam-bad-odds-11640706082?page=1

Chapter 1: Angels Still Appear in Prisons

1. Annie Fourcaut, "Les banlieues populaires ont aussi une histoire," Revue Projet 2007/4 (n° 299), pages 7 à 15, https://www.cairn.info/revue-projet-2007-4-page-7.htm

Chapter 2: How My Years of Rebellion Started...

1. Centre Social Air Bel – Marseille, "Qui sommes-nous?," Air-Bel, 2023, https://www.csairbel.com/qui-sommes-nous/
2. Barbara Forey, Jan Hamling, John Hamling, Peter Lee, International Smoking Statistics – France, Sep. 17, 2009, http://www.pnlee.co.uk/Downloads/ISS/ISS-France_090917.pdf
3. van Reek J., Adriaanse H. and Karaoglou A. (1992). Smoking among children in the European Community. J Public Health Med, 14, 93-4.
4. "Children Exposed to Violence", National Institute of Justice. Sep. 21, 2016, https://nij.ojp.gov/topics/articles/children-exposed-violence
5. "Protection of children from the harmful impacts of pornography", UNICEF, 2021, https://www.unicef.org/harmful-content-online
6. Michael Shader, "Risk Factors for Delinquency: An Overview," Office of

Justice Programs, Jun. 9, 2020, https://www.ojp.gov/pdffiles1/ojjdp/frd030127.pdf

Chapter 3: My Family's Fight to Beat the Odds

1. Agnès van Zanten, "Schooling Immigrants in France in the 1990s: Success or Failure of the Republican Model of Integration?", Anthropology & Education Quarterly, Vol. 28, No. 3, Ethnicity and School Performance: Complicating the Immigrant/Involuntary Minority Typology (Sep., 1997), pp. 351-374 (24 pages), Published By: Wiley
2. Jacqueline Serrato, Pat Sier, and Charmaine Runes, South Side Weekly, "Mapping Chicago's Racial Segregation", Feb. 24, 2022, https://interactive.wttw.com/firsthand/segregation/mapping-chicago-racial-segregation
3. Elizabeth McGhee Hassrick, Stephen W. Raudenbush, and Lisa Rosen. (2017). The Ambitious Elementary School: Its Conception, Design, and Implications for Educational Equality, University of Chicago Press

Chapter 4: Struggling to Find Me in Two Different Worlds

1. "Émeutes dans les banlieues françaises depuis les années 1970", Wikipedia, 2023, https://fr.wikipedia.org/wiki/%C3%89meutes_dans_les_banlieues_fran%C3%A7aises_depuis_les_ann%C3%A9es_1970

Chapter 5: My Time to Rise from the Ashes

1. Casualty Actuarial Society (CAS) and Society of Actuaries (SOA), Be An Actuary, 2023, https://www.beanactuary.org/
2. "Dix ans après l'incendie criminel, L'Haÿ n'oublie pas les 18 morts de la tour 2", Le Parisien, Sep. 3, 2015, https://www.leparisien.fr/val-de-marne-94/dix-ans-apres-l-incendie-criminel-l-hay-n-oublie-pas-les-18-morts-de-la-tour-2-03-09-2015-5059793.php

Chapter 6: Pursuing My American Dream: Become a Fellow Actuary

1. "University Mission Statement," DePaul Division of Mission & Ministry, Mar. 4, 2021, https://offices.depaul.edu/mission-ministry/about/Pages/mission.

aspx

2. "Our Mission," IABA – International Association of Black Actuaries, https://www.blackactuaries.org/

3. Society of Actuaries, "Pathways", 2023, https://pathways.soa.org/

Chapter 7: I Almost Fell Back; I Almost Gave Up

1. The Infinite Possibilities Conference, "Building Diversity In Science," http://www.diversityinscience.org/infinite-possibilities-conference/

Chapter 8: But God Picked Me Up!

1. Chris Isidore, "The Great Recession's lost generation," CNN Money, May 17, 2011,

2. https://money.cnn.com/2011/05/17/news/economy/recession_lost_generation/index.htm

3. Coursera, 2023, https://www.coursera.org/

4. John Phillips, "Why your kids will want to be data scientists", CNBC, Jun. 3, 2014, https://www.cnbc.com/2014/05/30/why-your-kids-will-want-to-be-data-scientists.html

Chapter 9: The Final Stretch to Becoming a Fellow Actuary

1. Society of Actuaries, "Diversity, Equity & Inclusion," 2022, https://www.soa.org/programs/diversity-inclusion/data/

2. United States Census Bureau, "QuickFacts United States", 2022, https://www.census.gov/quickfacts/fact/table/US/RHI225221

Conclusion: Purpose Is Calling

1. The Actuary Magazine, "Persevere With Passion – Q&A with Rolande Sonya, ASA, MAAA, Managing Actuary, Health Care Service Corporation," Apr. 28, 2020, https://www.theactuarymagazine.org/persevere-with-passion/

2. Ellyn Fortino, "San Miguel School's Austin campus slated to close," Austin Weekly News, May 2, 2012, https://www.austinweeklynews.com/2012/05/02/san-miguel-schools-austin-campus-slated-to-close/

Acknowledgments

———

I would have never achieved so many heights in my life and career without the love and support of many people God used to support and bless me.

To the loves of my life, my husband, Gbenga, and our lovely children. Thank you for the love and patience you have shown me during this journey of becoming a Fellow Actuary and writing this book. Thank you for walking alongside me to fulfill my life's purpose joyfully. God's Hand is so mightily upon our family; He mercifully guards us.

To my mom. I would not be where I am today if you had not been as gracious as you have been toward me. I was a difficult child to raise, but you never stopped believing in the potential God placed in me. You saw me beyond my errors, and I am forever grateful for that. Only God could repay your investment and endless sacrifice to see me where I am today. It is with tears of thanksgiving and admiration for you. Mom, that I thank you. You inspire me.

To my dad. You have always believed in my ability to succeed as an Actuary. It didn't matter how many exams I failed; you always planted in me that I was a genius (just like you, haha). Thank you for modeling so well the importance of education. I thank God for the grace you had to work so tirelessly to open doors of opportunities for our family to move to France and the United States. You inspire me to rise higher for the next generations.

To my siblings. Thank you for supporting me financially in my season of wilderness and never judging me when I was at my lowest or in my rebellious phase. You have always cheered me on to rise higher. I have prayed with all my heart for God to bless you beyond measure!

To my aunt Christine. Thank you for introducing me to the actuarial profession and welcoming me into your home when I moved to the United States. I fulfilled your dream by becoming a Fellow Actuary, and I thank you for believing from day one that I could do it.

To my aunt Catherine, of blessed memory. Thank you for opening your home to me when I moved to the United States. You always treated me and cheered for me like your own daughter. You literally have celebrated all of my successes and stood by me without judgment when I felt like a failure. I will forever cherish the laughter and camaraderie I had with you.

To my high school principal and teachers, I am so thankful to God for how gracious and patient you were with me. Thank you for believing in my family and pushing me to work hard in academics. You helped set the proper foundation for my career journey.

To my DePaul University professors and leaders, thank you for believing in me, financially investing in me, and giving me a passion for service to others. I am forever grateful for having attended DePaul.

To my past and present professional mentors and managers, you have inspired me to pass the torch to others and set the proper legacy for me to follow. Thank you for your time guiding me in my career and believing in my ability to become a Fellow Actuary.

To the International Association of Black Actuaries (IABA). Thank you for inspiring me and making my vision to become a Black Fellow Actuary so real and possible. To all IABA leaders, you have birthed what generations ahead of us will forever be grateful for.

To my high school and university classmates and coworkers with whom I spent countless hours studying for school exams or actuarial exams, thank you for the motivation you gave me not to give up and to keep dreaming high. Your moral support kept my career dreams alive!

My profound thanks to my spiritual mentors and destiny friends! I thank God for using you to help me realign my destiny towards a greater purpose and for making sure that I don't drift back but keep moving forward. More specifically, thank you for praying for me to find the drive to write while being a young mother and for encouraging me throughout the entire process until the vision for the book was accomplished.

To my book editing and design team, thank you for working alongside me with excellence to bring the vision of this book to life. Thank you for your diligence and touch of perfection. May God increase and prosper all the works of your hands.

BEAUTY
DELIVERED

NO MORE ADDICTION, NO MORE SHAME

Sonya Rolande

Foreword by BAYO ADEWOLE

Beauty Delivered

In her first book, Sonya shares her full personal testimony of how she became a Christian and how Jesus led her during a difficult season in discovering her life's purpose.

Available now on Amazon

Let's Stay Connected!

www.ingramcontent.com/pod-product-compliance
Lightning Source LLC
Chambersburg PA
CBHW050855150626
46549CB00013B/1893